10-Minute
Life Lessons
for Kids

10-Minute Life Lessons for Kids

52 Fun and Simple Games and Activities

to Teach Your Child Trust, Honesty, Love, and

Other Important Values

Jamie C. Miller

ILLUSTRATIONS BY CAM CLARKE

HarperPerennial
A Division of HarperCollinsPublishers

HarperCollins books may be purchased for educational, business, or sales promotional use. For information please write: Special Markets Department, HarperCollins Publishers, Inc., 10 East 53rd Street, New York, NY 10022.

FIRST EDITION

Designed by Elina D. Nudelman

Library of Congress Cataloging-in-Publication Data

Miller, Jamie C.
    10-minute life lessons for kids : 52 fun and simple games and activities to teach your child trust, honesty, love, and other important values / Jamie C. Miller. — 1st ed.
        p. cm.
    Includes bibliographical references.
    ISBN 0-06-095255-5
    1. Child rearing. 2. Moral education. 3. Values. 4. Children— Conduct of life. 5. Active learning. I. Title.
HQ769.M5327 1998
649' .1—dc21   98-18484

        02 ❖/RRD 10 9 8 7 6

To my father, whose life was the ultimate lesson

Contents

Contents

Contents

Contents

Acknowledgments

To my mother, Donna Conkling, for putting life into life, and the heart into our home.

To my father, Jim Conkling, whose entire life taught so many the real meaning of goodness.

To my children, Ryan, Seth, Kelly, Ian, and Alex, for holding my hand while I stumbled my way through the most holy of callings.

To Mike, for listening, for helping me turn thoughts into words, and for cooking dinner.

To Wilma and Frank Miller, whose example has taught me so much about loving children.

To Candy, Chris, Xan, and Laurette, for their unwavering love and support.

To Ben and Nancy Dominitz, for their wisdom, and for opening my eyes to the exciting world of publishing.

To Jennifer Basye Sander, for inspiring me to stretch and grow.

To my superb agent, Sheree Bykofsky, and her assis-

Acknowledgments

tant, Janet Rosen, for their extraordinary work on my behalf.

To my editors, Kate Ekrem and Kristen Auclair, for their gentle guidance from beginning to end.

To the many fine people at HarperCollins, for their confidence in this book.

To the many friends, religious leaders, and teachers I have had the privilege of working with throughout my life, for showing me the way.

Introduction

My son Ryan was 3,000 miles from home and didn't know anyone. Unlike many of his good friends who had chosen to go to college close to home in California, he had decided to go to the University of Virginia. I had gone with him and had spent a couple of days getting him settled in his apartment, but as the hour for me to leave for the airport arrived, we were both feeling the loneliness of his new surroundings.

I tried to keep my composure by giving him last-minute instructions and advice about doing laundry, grocery shopping, and other mundane aspects of life on his own. Then, just five minutes before I had to drive away, he asked me to quickly show him how to sew a button on a shirt. So through tears now visibly running down my cheeks, I tried to thread a needle and demonstrate the task for him, with tears now running down his face also. In retrospect, it was a very funny scene, but the experience made me wonder, during my long return flight, what other things I hadn't taught him in his 18 years at home.

I suppose all parents have similar nagging feelings when their children leave the nest. But the questions that tug most at your heart aren't the ones about whether you taught your child how to sew on a button or change a tire on his car or the sheets on his bed. They are more likely to be questions like "Did I teach him his manners and how to be respectful of others? Did I let him know how extraordinary he is and treat him with the respect that builds self-confidence? Did I teach her how to set goals and set priorities, and to persevere until those goals are realized? Did I teach her how to deal with disappointment and loneliness? Did I teach him that he can make a difference in the world? Did I teach him that getting along in the world is much more important than getting ahead? Did I teach her that the real joy in life comes from serving others? Did I do too much for her and not enough with her? Did I not say enough, or did I say too much and listen too little?"

Most of us, when that time comes, won't be able to avoid the feelings that we somehow could have been better parents—that we could have done more, could have been more effective, more loving, more perceptive, or could have been better examples to our children. But we will have more peace of mind if we know we have at least passed on to them a few of the most important things in life—the values that will help them become successful, competent, caring, and ethical adults.

The desire of most parents is first and foremost to do what is best for their children. No one tries to be a bad parent; all parents want their kids to be happy. In fact, when parents make mistakes, it's not usually because they don't care, but because they care so much.

One of the best ways to raise children who will end up being happy, productive adults is to give them a moral code by which to live—a firm foundation of beliefs that will give them the inner guidance needed to make choices and face challenges in life. As the country song says, "You've Gotta Stand for Something, or You'll Fall for Anything." Children look to their parents to stand for something—to set boundaries, establish rules of behavior, and point them in the right direction.

Who Should Teach Values?

Several years ago in Southern California, Tom and Pauline Nichter and their 11-year-old son, who were homeless and jobless at the time, found a wallet containing about $2,400 in cash, a credit card, and an airplane ticket. They immediately turned it in to the police, who were grateful but also surprised by the couple's unhesitating explanation that they "were just doing what we were brought up to do—being honest."

As the media became aware of the situation, people around the country watching the news coverage were astounded at this extraordinary act of integrity. The owners of the wallet were found, but then an amazing thing happened. The Nichters started receiving letters—boxes and boxes of letters with donations of every size, job offers for both of them, and notes from complete strangers volunteering to help find housing for the family. People all over the country were so inspired by this family's honesty that they sent in a total of over $16,000 in donations. At one point, as Pauline Nichter stood in the midst of the bundles of letters coming in to the police station, she laughingly remarked, "This is all my mother's fault."

"This is all my mother's fault." In that one sentence, a whole lifetime of one mother's devotion, teaching, and example had been sufficiently rewarded. And at the same time, the morals which that mother had so profoundly instilled in her daughter, Pauline, were being passed down to yet another generation. Eleven-year-old Jason stood beaming before the cameras, holding his mother's hand, obviously proud of the parents he would always be able to look to for clarity in a world full of moral confusion.

There's not much debate anymore about who should teach these important principles to our children. Schoolteachers are no longer allowed to teach them, or lack the time, energy, or parental support for such programs. Churches provide some very fine moral instruction, but don't reach enough people. The obvious answer is that values need to be taught by parents within the family setting.

There are many forces in the world today that pull against the family unit, but it is still the basic institution of society. The government may create organizations to take the family's place, our society may try in vain to create agencies to reform those who are delinquent, but nothing can replace the influence of the family. How much better it is to shape a human being from birth in a loving family than to try to reshape him later when his life has fallen apart because his family didn't care. As the child psychologist Dr. Kevin Steede has said, "It's not a question of if you're going to parent, it's a question of when. Pay the price now with your time and attention, or pay the price later for expensive rehabilitation."

There is no more important work in your life than the work you'll do at home. It has been stated, "If we all work on all the problems in our society and forget the fundamental unit of the family, it would be analogous to straightening deck chairs on the *Titanic*." It is in this laboratory of life, the laboratory of our homes, that we learn life's most important lessons. It is with the people with whom we spend our days and our nights, our most intimate moments, our most difficult moments, that we have the potential of developing the most meaningful relationships. It is in our "home school" that our character is tested most and therefore can experience the greatest growth.

Most families are less than perfect; there is rivalry and contention, sometimes abuse and pain. Not all homes are conducive to warm, cozy evenings by the fireplace talking about trust or love. Some families won't feel comfortable doing some of the activities in this book together. But one way or another, we must teach this basic "goodness" to our children. Just as a great baseball player has to continually practice baseball, children have to be given the opportunities to practice goodness if they are to develop the habits of goodness. Perhaps for families who are really struggling, a parent can teach these principles one-on-one with his child in quiet moments. If we can take just a few minutes here and there to gently guide our children toward becoming selfless, respectful, resourceful, and compassionate people, then our home will be a school whose graduates will someday be depended upon by all of society.

The Maze of Life

On a very hot summer day a few years ago, I took my three youngest children to an amusement park that contained a giant outdoor maze. It had several miles of paths to wander through before you could find your way out of it. The paths were lined on both sides with 10-foot walls to prevent you from seeing anything except what lay directly in front of you. Some people are able get through the maze in 15 minutes or so, and some people get stuck in there for more than an hour.

At three or four strategic points throughout the maze, there are stairs leading to higher ground—lookout platforms of sorts—for those frustrated or unpretentious souls who surrender to "cheating" occasionally to get their bearings. You will also notice little clusters of tired mothers and fathers perched atop these platforms—some shouting directions to their children to speed up the trek, others watching the process with intrigue and enthusiasm, and still others bored, annoyed, or flatly resigned to waiting out the routine.

As I made my way among these klatches of parents and observed the vast array of behavior of both the children and adults, it was suddenly clear that the scene before me was a rather fitting metaphor for life in general, or, more specifically, the relationship between parent and child. I had three kids down below in the maze; I had a long time to think.

There were all kinds of children and all kinds of parents. There was the group of kids who were running and laughing, enjoying every minute of their fun adventure—wanting to stay till the park closed, and not concerned in the slightest about whether they ever found their way out. They were there for the "ride," living in the present, not too worried about "succeeding," and oblivious to the time or the finish line.

Then there were the children who were very deliberate about the process. They were analytical, scientific, using their brains and their logic to find the best solution to the puzzle. Like the rat sniffing its way to the cheese at the end of the maze, they carefully plodded their way along, looking in all directions, depending on all five senses to find their way out. These were the children who enjoyed the challenge of the journey.

Some children seemed to have a sixth sense about finding the right path. They were the "naturals"—the ones who needed very little coaching because their instincts seemed to lead them in the right direction. They were the ones whom the rest of the world would refer to as "having it easy."

There were other types of children, too. There were those who didn't have any parents with them and were left to figure things out for themselves, whether they liked it or not. They had no voice to follow except their own internal compass. Sometimes it led them in the right direction and sometimes it didn't.

There were children who were reckless. They darted from path to path without regard for anyone or anything around them. They seemed to be distracted, confused, frustrated by the complicated course and anxious to get the whole thing over with. They didn't see any joy in the journey and were looking for the easiest escape.

The parenting styles I observed that afternoon also ran the gamut. There were parents who wanted be a part of the process every inch of the way– hoping to control every move their children made. They saw the maze as a race and seemed worried and anxious that their children might not have the drive to finish first. There were parents whose natural concern caused them to conscientiously guide and direct their kids along the right path. They wanted to prepare their children by pointing out warning signs and stumbling blocks along the road. Although they were well aware that their children would encounter some occasional setbacks, they wanted to help them avoid the major ditches and detours that could cause a serious delay or breakdown.

I saw some mothers reading books or painting their fingernails. They would take an occasional glance up, keeping an obligatory eye on the situation, but seemed too self-absorbed to get very involved in the process taking place below them. I saw a few fathers who had the look of science professors standing back and observing their experiments below. They seemed aloof, if somewhat intrigued by the procedure, determined not to interfere with the spontaneous outcome of their kids' choices. There were parents who looked like they were almost scoffing at their kids' confusion, parents who seemed angry because their kids were taking too long, and parents whose eyes had a hopeless look that made me think the job of parenting had worn them out completely.

And, of course, there were plenty of parents happy to

be spending a day of genuine fun and adventure with their children. I suppose the thing I came away with that day was that each of these parents, in their own way, was doing his or her best. All of us, according to our own background, experience, and ability, have strengths and weaknesses that determine our effectiveness as parents. As we face the incredible challenge of raising all different kinds of children, all with their own strengths and weaknesses, we try to find the right balance in the methods we use to teach and train them.

Like the maze, life for our children is confusing at times. Some children are better equipped than others to deal with the detours, the sudden changes in direction, and the opportunities at the end of the road. Some will move full steam ahead, confident of their destination, and others will dawdle along the winding road at a much slower rate. Some will need a lot of our help along the way, and others will be fairly successful if they just follow their own noses. But all children, regardless of their natural temperament, their talent or intelligence, need some basic guidance from good parents steering them in the right direction.

No-Guilt Parenting

Accepting the major responsibility for teaching our children these important principles causes many of us anxiety. Sometimes we're not even sure that we, as adults, have a handle on all the implications of abstract concepts like empathy, resourcefulness, and loyalty. Then, when we find ourselves with a sudden case of road rage while driving on the freeway to work, or catch ourselves telling a little fib to the salesman at our front door, we even begin to question our ability to effectively teach our kids about the virtues of things like courtesy, patience, or honesty. In many ways, parenting forces us to get to know ourselves a little better than we might like. So for some parents, the whole issue of teaching family values adds up to simply one more thing to feel guilty about—one more thing we're supposed to be doing as a parent, but can't for the life of us figure out how or when to do.

We all need to lighten up! The constant anxiety so many of us feel over "being an effective parent" can end up being very counterproductive. If we are continually berating ourselves for not living up to our idealized images of successful parents, we will miss out on the deeply rewarding joy of caring intensely for another human being—the exhilaration that comes from watching that bright, cheerful, creative, inquisitive, and funny child grow and flourish. It has been said that "being a parent is such serious business that we dare not take it too seriously." We need to be kinder and gentler to ourselves, to be human and honest, and to learn to laugh at our mistakes.

The journalist and author Mary Kay Blakely has said, "We all have bad days, of course, a secret that only makes us feel more guilty. But once my friends and I started telling the truth about how far we deviated from perfection, we couldn't stop. . . . One mother admitted leaving the grocery store without her kids—'I just forgot them. The manager found them in the frozen foods aisle, eating Eskimo Pies.'"

Fortunately, children don't need perfect parents. They are remarkably resilient creatures and, with a little direction, can turn out to be great kids in spite of our mistakes. Some days, however, we even question our ability to give that "little direction." As we race from the office to gymnastics, Little League, a quick stop at the library, an all-too-familiar drive through the golden arches, and on to what awaits us at home—helping with homework, doing the laundry and the dishes, and preparing for the next day—we wonder whether our family is heading in any meaningful direction, or whether we're teaching our children much of anything along the way.

We find ourselves wondering how the family down the street manages to have such perfectly manicured lawns, cars that are always clean, and two perfectly mannered and perfectly coiffed daughters, who are also proficient at different musical instruments, are straight-"A" students, and are the most caring and responsible baby-sitters on the block. When we find ourselves secretly wanting to eavesdrop on that family to observe the methods used by their "superparents," it's good to remind ourselves of the words of the author Marianne E. Neifert, who puts it all in perspective: "The truth is, most of our alleged superheroes make meals, make beds, make ends meet, make mistakes, make amends, make love, make up, and mostly make do."

We need to remind ourselves that the job of parenting is a business of long-term rewards; in the short term, everything seems to be changing, nothing is ever finished, and most of the time you wonder if you're accomplishing anything of substance. And even if you think you're doing a decent job teaching your kids something of value from time to time, how do you measure the results? When can you write down in the baby book or journal, for instance, that your child learned to be truthful? Which day was it that she mastered compassion toward others? Was it on a Thursday or a Friday that he decided to take responsibility for his own actions? We finally have to come to terms with the fact that our daily workload as parents has to be counted as a process and not as a product.

So after all that, why do we need another parenting book telling us what we should be doing? Because this book won't add to the guilt. You won't feel the self-reproach for not doing what's in this book the way you do with so many parenting books, because it is simply so doable. There are no complicated charts, stars, or schedules, and even if you only open the book once a week or once a month or three times a year, your kids won't forget what they learn from these lessons. And after taking the little effort necessary to do these activities, you'll roll your tired body into bed with a smile, knowing that that day, at least, you spent 10 or 15 meaningful minutes with your children.

The Challenge of Teaching Values in Today's World

In the early 1950s a poll was taken among teachers across the nation, asking them to list the top five problems in their schools. The list:

Talking out of turn   Running in the hall
Chewing gum   Cutting in line
Making noise

In the early 1990s, teachers were asked the same question; some of their responses were to be expected, but the list was alarming nonetheless:

Drug and alcohol abuse   Suicide
Guns and knives in school Rape
Pregnancy

I don't need to enumerate all the frightening things going on in the world in which our children are being raised; we are well aware of the nation's moral decline over the past 30 or 40 years. Suffice it to say that our children will need to be equipped to deal with a world filled with moral ambiguity.

That's the bad news. The good news is that there are millions of young people today—the "twenty-something" and "thirty-something" generation—who are becoming parents for the first time and are taking the job seriously. As I have observed many of these enthusiastic new mothers and fathers, their commitment is as obvious as it is heartwarming. They seem dedicated to teaching their children correct principles and back-to-basics values.

It's encouraging to see this trend among so many today, even if their motivation stems from slightly unfortunate circumstances. It may be that this generation is feeling the effects of their own upbringing: they were the first group to experience the downside of two-income family life. They were the original latchkey kids who found out that "quality time" wasn't all it was cracked up to be—and almost half of them ended up as children of divorce. Now the one solid commitment they're determined to make is to their own children. Many of them feel their parents simply weren't there to teach them many of life's valuable lessons, and they don't want to repeat that mistake with their own families. These young parents seem to understand that there is a direct connection between behavior that is governed by moral values and eventual personal happiness. And because they want that happiness for their children, they are ready and willing to take responsibility for teaching those life lessons to them.

How This Parenting Book Can Help You

Even the best of parents, however, can become bewildered and intimidated by all the information available and all the many experts' opinions about how to raise children. It's easy to become confused about the rules and our roles. We subconsciously ache for the simpler times of *Father Knows Best,* when parents had clearly defined duties and expectations; but when we knock on the doors of America's neighborhoods, Ozzie and Harriet are seldom at home.

For all of today's families, in their varying configurations, the rules have changed. We're bombarded with new parenting theories, we take parenting classes, we read parenting magazines, we watch Oprah and all her authorities on the subject, and secretly wish we had just a glimpse at how their children have turned out, so we could decide which experts to believe.

The sagging shelves in the local bookstore's "Parenting" section have convinced us that we need to know not only how to parent but what to expect from children who are bright, unhurried, emotionally intelligent, playful, moral, creative, self-reliant, happy, unspoiled, well behaved, liberated, strong-willed, spiritual, spirited, and who have high self-esteem and no sibling rivalry. And after we've done all that with logic and positive discipline, at the same time giving them the love that heals and talking so they'll listen and listening so they'll talk, the experts finally tell us it's okay to be just a good-enough parent!

I'm not ungrateful for all these wise and well-meaning authorities. I have stacks of their books at home and have spent 20 years and a good portion of my family's income devouring their myriad philosophies. Before I was married, I had taken all the child development courses available in college and thought I was fully prepared to be a mother. I was certain my kids would be well behaved and talented and would go to Harvard on scholarships. I had the five ideas for raising children down pat. Then suddenly I was married, had five children, and no ideas. I still haven't figured much of it out, so I'm glad those folks keep writing books. But one thing is quite clear: what used to seem like a fairly natural and uncomplicated process called "childrearing" has turned into a full-time obsession, fraught with stress, self-doubt, confusion, and anxiety.

This book is not the solution to all those complexities

of parenting. It is not even intended to be a complete guide to teaching values to your child. If you're at the point where you're still wondering whether you should disapprove when your child mistreats another child, or whether you should discourage your child from cheating on a test at school, then there are other books to instruct you in the philosophy of virtue and essential family values. Read Aristotle, William Bennett, Stephen Covey, and many others for the basics.

While this book touches briefly on some moral common sense, it is mostly a practical tool to help reinforce the values you already hold dear. Naturally, teaching our children these important lessons is a lifelong process, most of it occurring automatically from the example we set as parents. But even though we attempt to "walk the talk" as consistently as possible, we will make some mistakes. None of us will be the perfect parent, so we need to find additional ways to help instill these principles in our children. The activities in this book will provide some of that assistance—they will stimulate children's thinking, generate some interesting discussion, and strengthen family ties all at the same time.

Show Is Better Than Tell

There has been much discussion in recent years about learning styles: some children are visual learners, some are auditory learners, some are kinesthetic learners. Actually, it has been found that learning styles are more of a developmental issue: a baby starts out by touching and putting everything in her mouth to learn about her surroundings—kinesthetic learning. As the child gets a little older, her visual ability becomes the key to her exploration of the world. And finally, she begins to assess her environment through auditory means. By the time she's an adult, she has probably incorporated all three styles, with some slight preference for one or the other.

However, when it comes to retaining the information absorbed in these three different ways, the old Chinese proverb says it best: "I hear and I forget; I see and I remember; I do and I understand." It is by doing something, participating, engaging all our senses, that we grasp the full meaning of what we're trying to understand. Learning usually takes place in the day-to-day experiences of living, shared moments of discovery, planned and unplanned events and activities, and stimulating hands-on adventure.

As parents, we often mistakenly equate teaching with talking. Forgetting that it's the least effective way to teach, we think we need to spell everything out to our kids, instruct them, explain every detail to them. But because they usually don't understand much of what we're talking about, they tune us out after the first few minutes of our lecture. In fact, it has been said that if you don't want your children to hear what you're saying, pretend you're talking to them.

I love the story of the mother who told her three-year-old she could ride her tricycle on the sidewalk out in front of the house, but that she could not ride past the corner. The little girl went out the door to play and, as her mother watched her, promptly rode her tricycle up and around the corner. The mother ran to catch up with her and scolded her for going past the corner. She again admonished, "You must not go past the corner. If you do it again, you'll have to come inside the house."

This time the little girl rode in front of the house for a few minutes and then, once again, went down the street and around the corner. Her mother again ran to her and in exasperation shouted, "Why did you disobey me? I told you not to go past this corner." The little girl looked up with big eyes and a quivering lip and asked, "But Mommy . . . what's a corner?" It never occurred to this mother that the words she kept repeating to her child were meaningless. Much of our parental lecturing is equally useless.

10-Minute Life Lessons for Kids is a book about seeing *and* doing—it will teach powerful principles without the child even realizing he is being taught—and without extensive lectures from the parent. Whether teaching about family unity, setting goals, or showing kindness to others, using the types of games and activities found in this book is one of the most effective ways to approach teaching these concepts. And because the activities include the use of tangible objects to teach intangible ideas, they will create a clear picture and leave a lasting impression on your child.

With these object lessons you can teach philosophical principles and emotions that are otherwise difficult to describe in words. Your children will discover the objectives themselves as they actively participate. Yes, there will be talking, but not lecturing. With questions, visual stimulation, and play, you'll be encouraging the child to draw his own conclusions—he'll be doing the talking, not you.

How to Use This Book

The activities in this book are intended to be used as a springboard for discussions with your children—to give you an opportunity to share your beliefs with them in a casual, creative, and fun way, and to give them a safe place to explore their own feelings about those beliefs. Not every activity will work for your family; the book is intended to be a source to dip into. Flip through the pages—mix and match whatever intrigues you and feels right for your particular family.

Many of the simple games in this book can be done riding in the car to soccer practice or sitting in the waiting room at the dentist's office. Most take 10 minutes or less. Some can be expanded to fill a whole evening of cozy family fun and togetherness, if that's the goal. Some take a few minutes of preparation ahead of time to be effective. There is no set schedule nor complicated plan to follow. They can be done once a week, once a month, or—even more effectively— whenever your child is struggling with a particular problem. You also might consider having a child be the "teacher" for some of the activities; many of them are simple enough for a child to demonstrate to the rest of the family.

The book consists of four or five activities for each of the 12 principles, and each game is contained on one or two pages; you only need to read those few pages to have a successful experience. The activities can be done in any order and can be chosen at random, or you can concentrate on one principle at a time and do several activities to underscore that value. You will need very few supplies. Just open the nearest junk drawer and you'll have almost everything you need at your fingertips: pennies, string, toothpicks, a candle, a balloon, sewing thread, popcorn, a newspaper, a ruler.

One of the challenges parents face is coming up with learning activities that hold the interest of different-aged children. The lessons in this book can be analyzed and discussed on many different levels and can be adapted for most ages. Very young children will learn basic principles, while older children and teenagers will gain new insights into familiar concepts. Even the parents who get involved will see things with a fresh perspective as they learn from their kids' thinking. These "visual metaphors" will leave a lasting impression on everyone who participates.

At the end of the book is a section called "Words to Live By." These mottoes are intended to be cut out of the book and posted on your refrigerator or bulletin board, to remind you and your children of some of the values you have discussed. The ones for parents can be posted on your bathroom mirror (or wherever), because they are more apropos for parents than for kids. You should put up only one at a time and leave it there for several weeks to allow the message to sink in and perhaps be committed to memory. These maxims may seem superfluous, but I would encourage you to use them. This is one book you have permission to cut up.

As we pore through the volumes of literature on child-rearing, we usually find that we can absorb only a limited amount of information and can remember even less. Even when we read an exceptional book cover to cover, we're lucky if, a month later, we're able to recall more than five or six significant points. Making use of the "Words to Live By" pages will provide a constant reminder of some of the important principles of parenting. And for your children, these easy-to-remember sayings will provide a "moral memory bank" on which they can draw whenever the need arises in their lives.

PART ONE

Priorities and the Things We Value

For the children:

The best things in life aren't things.

For the parents:

We have been so anxious to give our children what we didn't have that we have neglected to give them what we did have.

My parents' fiftieth wedding anniversary was approaching and we had been planning the celebration for months. A wonderful program had been arranged with special tributes, a slide presentation of their life together, and several different musical numbers. The climax would be at the end of the evening, when each of their 23 grandchildren, to the music of "Sunrise, Sunset" from *Fiddler on the Roof,* would walk up one by one and present their grandparents with a rose and a kiss. It would be an evening to remember for our whole family. Then came the call from Kevin.

Kevin was my son Ian's best friend. It was summertime and Kevin's family was going to stay at a beach house in Santa Cruz for a week and he wanted Ian to come along. They had a full week of fun planned, including the rides at the boardwalk and rented jet skis. As fate would have it, the beach trip fell during the same week as the anniversary party. Feeling troubled about the situation, Ian had to make the difficult choice between two good things.

We talked with him about choices, priorities, and the value of family. With a little encouragement, he made the somewhat painful decision to miss the beach vacation and go to his family gathering. He realized how important the celebration was to his grandparents, and knew there would probably be other opportunities to go to the beach. It wasn't an easy decision to give up such a fun time for something that seemed more like an obligation, but he now has wonderful memories of being with his cousins and grandparents, and feels that he made the right choice.

In a world that places so much value on success, wealth, beauty, fame, and acquiring "stuff," kids can become pretty confused about what is really important in life. In our materialistic society, it's hard to convince kids that people matter more than the clothes they wear and the cars they drive, that family experiences might be more important than activities with friends, or even that devoting the time to learning how to play a musical instrument might be more gratifying than simply buying another CD or tape. As one father said, "Things were different when I was a boy. My son's room has a color TV, a VCR, a CD player, and his own telephone. Now when I punish him, I have to send him to *my* room!" In recent years parents and teachers have been teaching kids to "just say no" to everything, it seems, except all the stuff they want to keep acquiring. Convincing kids (and adults) that the "best things in life aren't things" is, today, a very hard sell.

A single mother of three, Susan Wolford, expressed real frustration around Christmastime. She was feeling overwhelmed by the number of things her three children, ages 7, 10, and 12, had put on their "wish lists"—all the toys, games, sports equipment, and electronic devices they had seen advertised so exhaustively over the past few months, plus a list of clothes, shoes, and personal items they felt they *had* to have. Money was tight that year, but she knew how disappointed her children would be if they only received two or three of their desired gifts.

Susan had overheard her children talking to their friends last Christmas as they all compared what they got, and she sensed as she listened that the Wolford family had come up short once again. All of that deepened the nagging feeling that her family was getting too caught up in the commercialism of the holiday and was missing the true spirit of the season. She feared they were focusing on "the thick of thin things." Susan had posted a quote up on the fridge—"Measure your wealth not by the things you have, but by the things for which you would not take money"—and realized that her children would never appreciate the significance of that statement unless she initiated a change in their experience. So, in an effort to do things differently this year, she gathered her family together one night in late November and played Bare Necessities.

1

Bare Necessities

Group size: 2 or more

Age: 5–adult

Materials: blackboard or large sheet of paper, chalk or pencil

*T*his activity can be done with one child, a whole family, or a classroom. Sit down with the child or gather the family members together and ask the question, "Other than air, water and sun, what are some things that would be hard to live without?" (With older children the question might be phrased, "What are some things that make life worth living?") Go around the circle, and as each person responds, list his or her items on a blackboard, poster-board, or large sheet of paper.

As the list grows, and if the children have only come up with tangible objects such as toys, TV, and clothes, try to suggest some items that are meaningful to them such as friends, family, love, etc. You might ask, "What are other things that help you through the day?" or "What things make you feel good during the day?" Each family's list will be different, but the following are some ideas to get you started—there are hundreds of others:

TV	video games	VCR
toys	soap	stores
dishwasher	toothbrush	swimming pool
pencils	school	trampoline
house	washing	skis
bed	machine	piano
computer	makeup	glasses
paper	clothes	medicine
bike	mirror	tennis racquet
refrigerator	money	movies
car	love	learning
fire	blow dryer	friends
food	furniture	air conditioner
toaster	shoes	telephone
electricity	music	soccer ball
heat	family	jewelry
books	church	teachers

After you have generated a list, ask them to take turns crossing out one item they could live without if they had to. At first this will be easy, but as they get down to the more basic elements of life, it will become more difficult. There are no right or wrong answers to this—accept anything each person suggests he or she could seriously live without. Continue the exercise until there is only one item left. It will be fun for small children to realize what's really important to them, and thought-provoking for teens and adults. It's also fun to have the children explain their reasoning for removing each item.

Although it's possible that the last thing to be crossed off the list will be the swimming pool, or money, the last item could be something like family, friends, learning, or love. Depending on your comments and questions, it's possible to steer the kids to these kinds of conclusions. This game will automatically lead to some good discussion about your family's values and priorities. Try to make the children understand that "things" are not what bring true happiness and security in life.

Susan was surprised at some of her kids' answers. For one thing, she realized how important music was to them, as it was one of the last things to remain on the list. She decided to make an effort to expose them to a variety of music at home, and to see about getting tickets to an occasional community theater musical production.

Susan also hadn't realized how much her children wanted a computer, and how "out of it" they felt without one. She silently resolved to budget her money and make that her next major purchase. And finally, she was gratified to see that after much discussion and friendly feuding, "family" was the last item remaining on the board. A week later, she conducted one of the other activities in this section and then proposed her plan to the kids.

Through her church, Susan had gotten the name of a family who wouldn't be having any Christmas that year. They had two small children and the father had lost his job eight months earlier, and even putting food on the table was becoming a challenge for them. Susan suggested to her children that they give up a small portion of their own Christmas in order to provide one for this needy family. The kids were reluctant at first, but the more they discussed it and how much fun it would be to do it secretly, the more excited they became. For several days, Susan's family shopped for toys and clothes to fit both of the children and then wrapped each one and signed the tags "From Your Secret Santa."

On Christmas Eve, they quietly placed all the gifts on the doorstep to the family's house, gave a few shakes on their jingle-bells, knocked on the door, and then ran and hid behind trees and bushes to await the family's squeals of surprise and delight when they opened the door. Returning home to hot chocolate and donuts, they laughed and talked about how the children would feel the next morning when they opened their gifts, and how the parents would always wonder who cared about them enough to do this anonymous kind deed.

Naturally, Susan's kids loved opening their own presents, too, the next morning. There may have been some slight momentary disappointment over the fact that not everything on their lists was there, but they seemed to feel the purpose of the sacrifice—they had given up some of their own desires to make a few other, less fortunate children happy. Susan even noticed that when they "compared notes" with their friends this time, all they wanted to talk about was their "secret Santa" escapade.

But the true spirit of the season touched her most when, in church a few days later, her children experienced the sweet joy of giving, as they noticed both of the children walk in, proudly wearing the new clothes that had been mysteriously delivered to their doorstep on Christmas Eve. Susan knew this would be a Christmas to remember, and felt that these simple games and discussions about the things that matter most had "opened the door" to this experience.

Try this experiment on your family: Ask any member to name one thing he got for Christmas last year or the year before. Now ask someone else to name one thing she got for her last birthday. In most cases, people can't remember too many of the *things* they receive as gifts. But ask any child if he can remember the time he secretly delivered gifts to another family or left cookies on a neighbor's doorstep, and he'll be able to tell you every detail, including his feelings about it. People generally remember experiences, not things, and experiences associated with emotion make lasting impressions. Nonmaterial gifts, thoughtful deeds, and acts of service are important events to a child, and as he learns to value them, he'll grow up with the desire to generate similar experiences for those around him.

As parents, we are often so anxious to give our children what we didn't have growing up that we neglect giving them what we did have. The five activities in this section help you talk with your family about establishing priorities with your time, your focus, and your finances. It will also help you discuss making wise choices and creating balance in life. Even very young children can grasp the fundamental concepts of this somewhat complex topic.

2

A Matter of Time

Group size: 2 or more

Age: 5 and up

Materials: clear glass jar (canning jar or mayonnaise jar); whole walnuts, Ping-Pong balls, or other similar-sized objects; rice, salt, or sugar; containers to hold walnuts and rice

*B*efore you begin this activity, fill the jar to the top with walnuts or whatever objects you're using. Pour the rice over the walnuts, filling in all the gaps to the top. Empty the jar and separate the rice and walnuts into two containers.

Begin by telling the children that the jar represents the amount of time available to all of them (you can label the jar with a sticker that says "24 Hours" if you want). Explain that the walnuts represent all their responsibilities and the "hard things" in their day (chores, homework, practice, etc.) and the rice represents the fun and easy things in their day (playing outdoors, watching TV, etc.). Ask one child to come forward and fill up his "day" with a mixture of as many hard and easy activities as he can fit in the jar. He will probably pour rice in first and then add some walnuts, but unless he puts all the walnuts in first, he will not be able to fit everything in the jar. Allow him to do it however he thinks best. Note that he was not able to accomplish all that he intended that day.

Pour everything out, divide the rice and walnuts again, and then demonstrate the alternate method, which will allow him to accomplish all he needs to and wants to in any given time period. Explain that by fulfilling our responsibilities (filling the jar with walnuts) and tackling some of the hard but important tasks in life first, there will always be time left over for recreation and fun (pouring the rice in to fill all the gaps). When we spend the first part of our day doing easy, unimportant things, it is a form of procrastination, and we are usually too tired or unmotivated to dig into the more challenging activities late in the day.

If a child happens to fill up the jar "correctly," point out why it worked and discuss the principles involved. This activity can easily be adapted for different age levels, and with older children, you can compare this to life in general—the priorities we set and the balance we attain in accomplishing our goals throughout the year.

3
Sweet Deceptions

Group size: 2 or more

Age: 3 and up

Materials: a ripe, juicy orange or apple (or 1 piece of fruit for each child); a candy bar for each child

This is a simple demonstration but it can lead to some good discussion about values and priorities in life. Simply show the children the orange and the candy bar (be sure to have a kind they like). Ask them individually which of the two items they would like. After each child chooses, ask him why he chose the one he did.

Next, give each child a piece of the candy or orange, depending on his choice. First speak to those who chose the candy bar, saying something like, "You have chosen the food that will give you quick energy. It is very sweet and delicious to eat. However, it doesn't last very long and it is mostly empty calories. A few minutes after you eat it, you'll be hungry for more."

To those who chose the orange say, "The orange will also give you energy and it is sweet to the taste. However, the orange has more nutritional value and will supply you with Vitamin C. You will feel more satisfied and benefit from the energy it gives for a longer period of time. The decision to take the orange was a wise one." Explain the value of both the orange and the candy, even if no one chooses one of them.

Now ask the children how you can compare the orange and candy bar to the decisions we are faced with in life. Accept their answers and their reasoning, adding your thoughts only if they miss the main point. You can point out that life is full of choices; many of the things we choose will bring us immediate pleasure but have no long-lasting value. Ask the children if they can name some of those kinds of choices. On the other hand, if we are wise, we will make the choices that will bring us a longer-lasting type of happiness and satisfaction. Think of some situations appropriate for the children's ages such as the ones below, and ask them to decide on the wisest choices for each scenario. You might also ask them to identify the immediate pleasure (like the candy) and the long-term satisfaction (like the orange) in each case.

- You are supposed to practice the violin for 45 minutes after school, but your neighbor invites you over to watch a new video instead.

- You have been saving your allowance for a new pair of in-line skates, but as you walk by an arcade, you think about spending your five-dollar allowance (in your pocket) on the arcade games.

- You're talking on the phone to your friend, and your mother asks you to make the salad for dinner. You've only been talking for ten minutes and don't want to get off yet.

- Your grandfather is sick in the hospital and your parents want you to go with them to visit him. You don't like the smell of the hospital and would rather go to the mall with your friends.

- Your school is putting on a science fair, and your teacher has told your class that doing a science project is a good learning experience, but that it is not required. You know your parents will want you to participate if they know about it. You consider not showing them the note about the fair, because you'd rather play basketball after school than work on a science project.

4
Weighing In

Group size:	2 or more
Age:	5 and up
Materials:	2 small Ziploc bags; wire hanger; 30–50 pennies; masking tape; pencil or pen; hook or nail

*L*abel two small Ziploc bags with a piece of masking tape; on one write "life's stresses" and on the other write "life's pleasures." Zip these onto the two opposite ends of the bottom of a wire clothes hanger; naturally you will not be able to zip them all the way, but that's okay. Suspend the hanger on a hook or nail, so it balances freely. Now you have your life scale.

Put a small square of masking tape on each penny. Help each member of the family mark his or her pennies with a word or abbreviation standing for each of that person's current activities (playing video games, swimming, piano lessons, watching TV, soccer), commitments (visiting friends and family, service activities, church, Boy Scouts), and daily responsibilities (school, chores, homework, job).

Let each person take a turn to discover whether or not her life is in balance. As she picks up one of her pennies, she should decide whether that activity or "weight of life" brings pleasure or pressure. Let each family member decide in her own mind how that activity makes her feel. After she has deposited all her "weights," it will probably be obvious if her life is in balance or out of whack.

This is a good time to discuss what the child could do to restore equilibrium in her life. Perhaps she needs to remove one or two of the sources of stress to make the other activities more pleasurable. Maybe it's as simple as limiting TV time. This is also a good time to talk about the fact that although some activities feel like pressure at the time (practicing the piano, doing homework), many of those things will eventually bring pleasure and satisfaction in life.

5

The Golden Egg

Group size: 4 or more (a group is best)

Age: 3 and up

Materials: colored Easter eggs or colored paper;
1 golden egg (made with colored
paper or paint); baskets or lunch
sacks; paper with score chart

*T*his game can be played several ways. It can be done at
Easter time as a regular outdoor Easter egg hunt, or
indoors with eggs cut out of colored paper. It can also be
done at any other time of year as a fun learning activity,
and the hidden objects can be colored-paper squares,
shamrocks, hearts, or whatever other shape you desire.
Depending on the size group, you need at least five different colors and at least 8 to 10 eggs for each child participating. I will describe how it would be done as a
regular Easter egg hunt, and you can adapt accordingly.

Prepare ahead of time a large number of Easter eggs
in at least five different colors (e.g., pink, blue, green,
yellow, orange). Prepare one golden egg, using gold
paint, glitter, or gold foil. Hide all the eggs and give each
child a bag or basket. Explain the rules of the game:

- This is an Easter egg hunt for points; the winner will be the one with the most points.

- Each color of egg is worth a different number of points, but only the leader (you) knows the value of each color at this point.

- There is one golden egg.

- After you begin gathering the eggs and have collected several, you can start trading with each other, according to what color eggs you think have the most value.

- After the game is over, the color values will be announced and the children can tally up their scores.

At the end of the game, show a paper or chart with the following points (or an adaptation):

Blue egg =   1 points
Green egg = 5 points
Yellow egg = 10 points
Pink egg =   20 points
Orange egg = 50 points
Golden egg = minus 100 points
Five of a kind = 100 points
All one color = 1,000 points
One of each color = 500 points
Most eggs = 100 points
Least eggs = 1,000 points

After you have determined the winner, sit down in a circle and discuss some of the following questions or related ideas:

- Is it better to know the value of something before you acquire it or experience it? Why?

- How do we learn the true value of things in life?

- What are some of the things the world considers to be of value?

- What do you consider to be the most important things in life?

- In what ways do you think the following statement is true? "Life is like a jewelry store in which robbers had entered, but rather than taking anything, they simply switched all the price tags. Things that had great value were cheapened, and things that were of no value appeared to be extremely valuable."

Every day our children will make choices about what is important to them in life; ultimately, the nature of their choices will determine the quality of their lives. It's critical that parents create opportunities for children to recognize their ability to make decisions and to understand the consequences that will follow. In the end, however, nothing speaks louder to a child than the example his parents set in making wise choices, setting sensible priorities in life, and establishing and abiding by a moral code for their family.

PART TWO

Potential and Self-Worth

For the children:

You can count the seeds in an apple, but you can't count the apples in a seed.

For the parents:

They may forget what you said, but they will never forget how you made them feel.

—*Carl W. Buehner*

A father of three recently told me about a night at their dinner table: "Seven-year-old Stephanie was taking a second helping of spaghetti and meatballs. She was picking out only the meatballs and we told her to take some pasta too. 'No,' she said, 'I only want the meatballs,' as she continued to search out the pieces. Finally five-year-old Jon, in exasperation, said, 'Stephanie, I don't care *what* Mister Rogers says—you're not *that* special!'"

And so it goes. Mr. Rogers notwithstanding, children at a very tender age are forced to come to terms with that fine line between the belief that they are the rarest gem on earth and the harsh reality that they may be as common as quartz.

As a parent, you've seen it: your daughter comes home from school and drops her books on the floor. She had studied so hard for her math test, she knew she was going to ace it. And yet when test time rolled around and the pressure got to her, she found it impossible to concentrate and failed the test. "Why am I so stupid?" she moans. After years of struggling with certain subjects in school, she has pronounced the sentence on herself and is resigned to the fact that she just couldn't cut it academically. Period.

We've heard such negative self-evaluations from all our kids: "Mom, I'm fatter than anyone in my class. . . . Why is my hair so boring? . . . Dad, how come Eli made the basketball team and I got cut? . . . My teacher yelled at me again when I ran out for recess. . . . My science project only got a 'third place.' . . . Why wasn't I invited to Nikki's birthday party?"

As parents, we are all too aware that the world can be pretty tough on our children. Everyday experiences with friends, teachers, and family members can knock them around and chip away at their self-esteem. And while our kids do their share of pushing *us* to (and sometimes *over*) the edge, it is still important to remember that we are the principal "mirrors" in our children's lives. They will glean a great deal of their self-image by what they see reflected in our eyes, and positive reflections produce positive self-images. Every child has something distinctive and wonderful to offer the world, and no one can unveil to a child his unique strengths and individual worth better than his parents.

The trick is to find a way—somewhere between carpooling, microwave dinners, eight hours at the office, and six loads of muddy wash—to squeeze in a word or two to let your kids know how delightful they really are. We've heard the phrase "Catch them doing something good." Sounds easy enough. But just when you walk into the kitchen determined to praise their valiant efforts, you're assaulted by cupboards and drawers left open, tennis shoes puddling on the floor, dried spaghetti stuck to the table, frozen pizza crusts crumbling on the counter, milk rings hardening inside six or eight glasses in the sink, and kids who, in spite of decent report cards, seem to have a vocabulary limited to just three words: "What's for dinner?"

As we resolve once again to focus on the positive with our kids, it's also important to keep in mind that each child develops at his own individual rate and with his particular style. Making comparisons between children, especially siblings, is destructive. The expectations we have for each of our children, which many times are born of our own past experiences, personal needs, or cultural values, become yardsticks by which we measure each child. Kids feel the force of those expectations and, unfortunately, rarely question them; instead, they begin to question *their* personal adequacy.

Gail Olsen, a mother of five, shared an insight that came to her one day while she was out in her rose garden. She has 75 rose bushes in all—a magnificent variety of colors and scents when they are in full bloom. But this day she was pruning. As she handled the tightly closed green buds, she envisioned what each would look like when it reached its full maturity—with shades of scarlet, coral-orange, taffy-white, soft pink, deep yellow, all bursting forth with the sweet fragrance of tea and fruit and spring bouquets.

The actual buds before her had no color, no scent, no velvety texture, and yet, would anyone dare say these rosebuds were an ugly sight to behold? These delicate, undeveloped beauties were not deficient, not inferior because they lacked color and fragrance; they were simply at different stages of maturity than the roses in full bloom. Likewise, all of our children hold within them all the splendor and richness of the most lovely flowers, though the metamorphosis will occur at different times and seasons for each child. Instead of comparing the buds to the full-grown blossoms or trying to force open the tight green skins before their time, we need to learn to rejoice in the potential and see the beauty of each phase—whether in our garden plants or in our children.

The child psychologist Lawrence Kutner puts it this way: "A child's self-image is more like a scrapbook than a single snapshot. As the child matures, the number and variety of images in that scrapbook may be far more important than any individual picture pasted inside it."

So on the occasions that surely come to every child when he doubts his inner strength and uniqueness—times that just plain leave him feeling like Forrest Gump in a world of rocket scientists—try some of the following activities to give him a new perspective on his value and personal worth.

6
An Apple a Day

Group size: 2 or more

Age: 5 and up

Materials: several apples, if possible of different sizes, colors, and shapes; knife

___

*S*how your child several apples, emphasizing the difference in size, color, and general outer appearance. One apple could even be old and shriveled or badly bruised. Cut one apple in half—not lengthwise, as you would normally do, but across the apple. Ask the child what she notices about the seed pod. Explain that all apples have a similar five-pointed star inside that holds the seeds. Cut a few other apples in half to demonstrate that regardless of the outer condition, all apples have the same perfect star of seeds inside. This demonstration can be done even if you have just one apple, although it would be slightly less effective.

Explain that people are like the apples. People differ in their outward appearance—they come in all different sizes, colors, shapes, and ages. But inside each of us are the same seeds of potential, of what we can become. This "star" inside each individual is what makes him or her special. Like the seeds inside the apple that can grow and become a blossoming fruit tree, each person has unique gifts and talents waiting to be developed, which, if properly nourished, will make that person extraordinary in some way.

This activity can also be used to discuss the fact that people shouldn't be judged by their outward appearance. Instead of looking at qualities like size, shape, color, beauty, or age in our friends, we should learn to look for their inner strength and goodness. This "looking beneath the surface" attitude doesn't always come naturally to kids (or adults), but this apple "picture" is worth a thousand words, and will plant a seed in the child's mind's eye.

Each family will get something different out of this activity, but the following are a few ideas for talking to younger children about this important concept.

For Younger Children

- What is special about you? (Begin a list of the child's good qualities to get him started.)

- What do you like to do that you would like to do even better?

- Do you know anyone who is not very pretty or handsome but who is very nice? Talk about some of the child's heroes (sports figures, movie stars, musicians, teachers, etc.) and discuss their various physical attributes (What color is their hair? Are they thin or fat? Do they have wrinkles or freckles? Are they tall or short?). Ask whether or not those things have any effect on their special talents and good qualities.

- What would it take for one of these seeds to become a big apple tree (soil, sun, water, air)?

- What kind of nourishment would it take for you to develop one of your special qualities (lessons, practice, belief in yourself, encouragement from others)?

For Older Children

- What do you think your special talents or gifts are? How can we help you develop these talents?

- Why is it important to feel good about yourself?

- Can you think of a time when you made a judgment about someone based on the person's outward appearance and then later found out you were wrong?

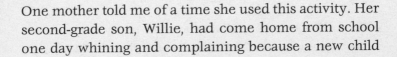

One mother told me of a time she used this activity. Her second-grade son, Willie, had come home from school one day whining and complaining because a new child had just joined his class. She was from another country and didn't speak English very well and Willie's teacher had placed her right next to Willie. He said the new girl dressed funny and that the kids made fun of her, and he felt stupid sitting next to her.

Although Willie's mother understood that his feelings were pretty normal, she thought it might be a good time to talk to him briefly about the difference between "looking good" on the outside and "being good" on the inside. She remembered the apple routine, showed it to Willie, and then asked him to try being friendly to the new girl for the next few days at school. And then each day for the next week, mom packed half an apple in Willie's lunch, star-side out. Willie told her later that each time he saw the seeds, he thought about their talk, and was finding it a little easier to be nice to the new girl, who, he had discovered, was a "whiz at math!"

7

The Worth of a Soul

Display the dollar bill and the pennies. Ask the child or children to examine them and try to discover all the ways the bill and coins differ. Accept their observations and add some of your own if they haven't been mentioned. The pennies are hard to the touch while the dollar bill is soft and flexible. The pennies make noise when dropped on the table, while a dollar dropped on the table is almost silent. The dollar is green; pennies are copper colored. Pennies are heavier than dollars. A penny is a different shape than a dollar. You can rip a dollar bill; you can't rip or break a penny. Dollar bills can become wrinkled, pennies can't. Remind them also that although there are many differences between the two items, both have the same worth and value.

Now relate this comparison of the bill and the coins to people. Ask the children to tell you some ways that people are different from each other. You can suggest ideas similar to those used with the pennies and dollar: Some people are hard to get along with, while others are more flexible. Some people are noisy and talkative; others are soft and shy. People come in many different colors, depending on their nationality. Some people are heavy and some are light; they come in all different shapes and sizes. Some people can become "broken" more easily than others (discouraged, sad, yielding to temptation). Some people are old and wrinkled while others maintain a youthful "shine."

If the hundred pennies and the dollar bill, despite their physical differences, are worth the same amount, what can we say about people? Discuss the idea that to be good and decent people, we each need to recognize the infinite worth of each and every human being. Ask the children to think of what that means in practical terms with regard to old people who act strange at times, family members who don't always do what we want them to, school friends who might not always be friendly, teachers who sometimes seem unfair, political figures with whom we disagree, or people from foreign countries whose customs we don't understand.

8
Stars and Space Stations

OLDER VERSION

Group size: 4 or more   *Age:* 10 and up

Materials: pad and pencil, matches (optional)

❖

YOUNGER VERSION

Group size: 2 or more   *Age:* 3 and up

Materials: one candle (optional), coat and hat

---

*T*his game can be played two different ways: one for younger children and another for those 10 years and older.

For a Family or Group of Older Children, Teenagers, or Adults

Have your family sit in a circle and put a lighted candle in the center. Turn down the other lights to set the mood.

Tell the group to imagine that they are all trapped in a damaged space station orbiting the Earth. The station has been struck by a random meteorite, which has destroyed the electrical system, and soon the remaining oxygen will be lost. The emergency shuttle must be launched immediately before all electricity and oxygen are gone, but the shuttle will only hold three people (adjust this number according to the group's size—it should be a number about half the size of the group).

Each person will take the candle and tell why she should be included with those who escape. She should explain what good things she has to give the world, what her plans are for her life, how she could benefit others, how much the others back on Earth are depending on her return, or whatever reasons she feels are important to be a survivor. This is an exercise to help members of your family think about their own talents and potential, so the idea is for them to talk honestly about their strengths, instead of concocting phony character traits or silly scenarios.

To keep the mood somewhat serious, you might take your turn first and tell your own story, perhaps resigning your position on the space shuttle in the end as the responsible leader. After you have done so, pass the candle to someone you can trust to set the pattern for the others around the circle.

Discuss some of the following questions with your family, if appropriate:

- Why was it hard to tell the good things about yourself?

- Do you think the person who said nothing or very little should be left behind?

- Have you ever thought of your life plans before? Have you considered how you might be important to others?

- Would you be willing to donate your heart or some vital part of your body at your death to keep some important scientist alive? A government official? A movie star? A popular musician? A young child or a grandmother?

- Do you think those who were selected to escape really had something to contribute to the world or were they chosen simply on the basis of their power of persuasion or their popularity?

For a Family with Mostly Younger Children (Aged Three to Nine)

Dress up as much as you can like a newspaper reporter, with a hat, a paper badge, an overcoat if you have one, notepad, and pencil. You can also use a microphone if you have one. The child or children are to be themselves, but are to pretend that they have just become very famous. Your job as the reporter is to interview each "star celebrity" and learn as much about her as you can. You should listen carefully and take notes as the child talks about herself in response to your questions.

- What is your full name?

- How many people are in your family?

- What is your favorite color?

- What is your favorite thing to eat? What do you hate to eat?

- If you had $100 what would you spend it on?

- What scares you the most?

- What things make you laugh?

- Name something that makes you feel sad.

- If you could have any wish come true, what would it be?

- What can you do really well?

- What is the best thing about how you look?

- What do you want to do when you grow up?

- What great thing did you do to become so famous?

This is a simple activity, but to your child, it is a few minutes of your undivided attention and an opportunity for her to think and talk about her good qualities. As you show your interest by taking notes and treating her like a celebrity, she'll know she matters to you.

9

Hidden Treasures

Group size: 2 or more

Age: 6 and up

Materials: large metal or plastic mixing bowl; several coins; pitcher of water; cellophane tape or clay

*B*efore you begin, *secure several coins to the bottom inside of* the bowl with clear tape or clay and place the bowl on a table. Have a child come up and stand next to the bowl and describe what she sees inside. Tell her that each of the coins represents a "treasure" in the child's nature or personality. You can even name each quality as you attach the coin or point to it in the bottom of the bowl— her artistic ability, her optimistic nature, her willingness to help others, her resourcefulness, her kindness toward animals, etc. All children have many positive qualities, and most children don't hear about them often enough. This is a good time and a fun way to make note of those things that make each child unique. If you're doing this with a group of children, you can talk about good qualities in general.

Now ask the child to slowly move away from the bowl, keeping her eye on it as she walks backward. Tell her to keep going until she can no longer see the coins at the bottom of the bowl. Have the child remain where she is standing. At this point, talk about the things in life that sometimes cause us to lose sight of our special qualities and think less of ourselves. Depending on the age of the child, these things might include critical teachers, unkind friends, sibling rivalry, difficulty with certain subjects in school, not measuring up to the "best" child on a sports team or in a dance class, parents' expectations, etc. You might even name specific things in the child's experience as she takes each step backward. Naturally, the qualities discussed can be greatly simplified for young children.

With the pitcher, pour small amounts of water into the bowl at a time. Each time you pour, name something or ask the child to name something that can help her see her positive qualities—her true self. These could include things like finding something she is talented in and developing that talent, spending less time on unimportant things and more time learning and growing, not comparing herself to the "best" in the group, doing nice things for others, making a personal "victory list"—writing down all her good qualities, associating with friends who recognize her strengths, reading stories about people who have achieved greatness in spite of weaknesses or handicaps, etc.

Eventually, when the bowl is full of water, the child will be able to see the coins once again—her own "hidden treasures" will be brought into view for all to see. (This optical illusion occurs when the bowl is full of water and the light bends so that the child is able to see the reflection of the coins.)

10
Pass the Popcorn

Group size: 2 or more

Age: 4 and up

Materials: unpopped popcorn, popped popcorn (freshly popped, if possible)

---

*S*how the unpopped popcorn to the child and let him examine the kernels. Ask him if it would taste good to eat. Ask him to smell it and tell you how it smells. Then ask what you would have to do to make it edible.

Now show the child the popped popcorn (or let him help you pop it). Ask him to tell you how it smells. Ask him to eat some and tell you how it tastes. Explain that when we apply heat to the corn kernels, they burst open into fluffy white or yellow "blossoms" of delicious popcorn.

With older children, ask them how this little demonstration can apply to our individual potential and talents if the unpopped kernels represent our undeveloped talents. What in life can be compared to the heat needed to make the popcorn burst open?

For younger children, explain that our talents or abilities (name specific talents of the child, such as his ability to play an instrument or a sport such as soccer or baseball, to draw or paint, to write stories, sing, dance, make other people laugh) are similar to the unpopped popcorn. If we don't do anything to develop those talents, they will remain hard, cold, useless kernels inside us. If we apply heat and energy to them (the energy needed to practice and develop the skill) they will burst forth and become useful to us. And along with benefiting us as individuals, they will bring pleasure (the smell and taste of the popcorn) to others around us.

Talk about each child's individual talents and how she can develop them. Ask if she thinks it's important to share her talents and abilities with others. What would happen if she only developed her abilities for her own purposes? To bring home this principle, show her or tell her about a rose bush that has never had flowers cut from it—has never "given away" any of its beauty, and then one whose flowers are regularly cut to give pleasure to others. It is only by giving things away that we continue to grow personally. The more we share with others, the more abundant our growth.

PART THREE
Attitude

For the children:

Problems are opportunities in work clothes.

—*Henry Kaiser*

For the parents:

The pessimist says, "I'll believe it when I see it." The optimist says, "I'll see it when I believe it."

—*Robert Schuller*

My grandfather was a dreamer. He didn't have a practical bone in his body, but his creative energy and lofty dreams filled him with such spirit and panache that he was irresistible and beloved by his wife and eight children, indeed, by all who knew him. One Christmas, Grandpa King gave each of his children a different musical instrument, taught them all how to play and sing, and gave birth to a family orchestra, which he proceeded to take on the road for the next ten or so years.

Because it was the Depression era, there wasn't much money to be made playing small concerts in churches and schools throughout the West, so his family enjoyed little security, living off the meager change collected at the concerts. Grandpa didn't care much about owning a home or having fancy clothes; the security he would give his family would come from experiencing real life, which for him included the pursuit of dreams in the world of music and art, literature, travel, nature, and beauty.

And so this Pied Piper eked out a living for his large family during the twenties and thirties, all the while exposing them to the richness of everything in life money *couldn't* buy. As his grown children reflected recently on the gypsylike existence of their childhood, one of his younger daughters remarked, "Do you remember those balmy, romantic summer nights, camping outside under the stars as a family, listening to Daddy teach us about the constellations in the sky and recounting the botanical terms for every tree and flower along the road as we drove? Do you recall the excitement of camping out week after week as we traveled?" To which her older, more practical sister replied, "Honey, we weren't camping. We were homeless!"

Exciting experiences and high adventure versus the despair of homelessness. The difference in perception— the difference in attitude. We all know our attitude can have a great effect on our success and happiness in life. William James said that we can alter our entire lives just by altering our attitude. And attitude is catching—it's like chicken pox. If you decide you want to catch chicken pox, you go to someone who has it and become exposed to it. Since children spend a great deal of their formative years "exposed" to their parents, they will "catch" most of their mental attitudes from them. While most parents are not consistently the perfect picture of optimism and enthusiasm, there are things we can teach our kids that will help them grasp the concept of positive versus negative thinking.

The motivational speaker Zig Ziglar compares the mind to a garden. When you plant corn in a garden, you don't raise potatoes. Whatever you plant will eventually come up. In the same way, when you plant negative thoughts in your mind, negative reactions and attitudes will be your harvest. In addition, when you plant corn, one seed doesn't produce one ear of corn; it produces lots of corn. Between planting and harvest there is a tremendous increase in the number of corn kernels. The mind works in the same manner; whatever you plant in the mind is going to come up multiplied: negative or positive thoughts will multiply to produce general negative or positive attitudes.

On the day in which his one-thousandth attempt to create an electric lightbulb failed, Thomas Edison was asked by a reporter, "Mr. Edison, how does it feel to have failed so many times?" It was an unexpected question for Edison, but he calmly replied, "Fail? I haven't failed at all. I now know one thousand ways *not* to make an electric light bulb." There are endless examples, like Edison's, that we can use to demonstrate to our kids the great things accomplished by people who have maintained a positive attitude.

While most of our kids' successes and failures won't have the same impact on the world as Mr. Edison's, they need to be taught that maintaining a positive outlook on even the inconsequential events in life will make them happier people.

A friend of mine had a daughter, Erin, who was on a losing basketball team at her junior high school. Her team had lost every game so far, and they only had four games left in the season. She was discouraged, as was every other girl on the team. They felt their chances of winning any of the remaining games were hopeless, and Erin wanted to quit the team now, before she was humiliated any further. She was complaining to her mother one day after practice, and her mother, instead of lecturing her, decided to show her the demonstration in Sink or Swim.

11
Sink or Swim

Group size: 2 or more

Age: 5 and up

Materials: clear glass bowl with water,
modeling clay (not Play-Doh)

*R*oll clay into four balls, three of them small and one a little larger (like small and big marbles). Drop each one into the bowl of water and watch them sink. Tell the children that each ball represents a person and that most people at certain times in their lives feel discouraged, burdened by life's problems, or lonely. Just like the clay balls, they will sink into a sad state of discouragement. With younger children, it's good to pretend the clay balls are individual people with names, and talk about why each person might be feeling low or dejected ("This is Sandy and her pet dog has just run away from home and she hasn't been able to find him . . . "). As you roll each ball before you drop it in the water, mention the fact that if we are all "rolled up" in ourselves, it is impossible to look outward and see other's needs.

Now take the larger clay ball out, and start reshaping it as you talk about changing your attitude. Mold it into the form of a simple canoe. Discuss how it's possible to help change others' attitudes about life just by changing our own attitude and being a positive influence on those around us. By stretching and shaping ourselves, by staying flexible and receptive to the feelings of those around us, we will be more likely to be in a position to help others in times of need.

Put the "boat" in the water and watch it float. Now take each of the small balls and put them inside the "boat." Ask the children what can happen when one person changes his attitude and decides to become more positive and hopeful. He can help lift the burdens of others and can be an example to them of the strength that comes with optimism.

✎

After this demonstration, Erin's mother asked how she might be the "canoe" that could rescue the members of her team from sinking. Erin wasn't sure at first, but after thinking about it for a while, she came up with a plan. She approached her uncle, who managed a local water slide/amusement park, and asked if he would be willing to allow 12 girls into the park for a greatly reduced rate, the total of which Erin and her mom would split. After he agreed, Erin called each of the girls and told them that if the team could win just *one* game out of the next four, they could all spend the day at the water slides at no cost to them. This seemed to boost the morale of the girls, as well as give them something to work toward; with new determination and diligent practice, they were able to win the second and third games in the last four.

12

Rocks in Your Socks

Group size: 2 or more

Age: 4 and up

Materials: small pebbles, small pieces of candy

Begin by giving each child a small piece of candy, preferably one that will last a few minutes as they suck on it. Now have them place a small pebble inside one or both of their shoes and put the shoes back on. With the candy in their mouths and the pebbles in their shoes, go outside with them and take a short walk or have them walk around the inside of the house several times.

After the walk, ask each child to talk about his or her experience. What did he feel during the walk? What was he thinking about? In most cases the child will dwell on the discomfort of walking and won't say anything about the good taste of the candy.

Ask the children how this can be compared to our experiences in life. Do we sometimes focus on the difficulties and problems we have (the pebbles and rocks) and forget about all the good things around us (the sweet candy)? What do we talk about more during the day—the things that bother and worry us or the beauty of the day and the nice things people do for us? Do we spend more time wanting things we don't have or being grateful for what we have?

To reinforce this idea you might show your children the proverbial half-empty/half-full glass demonstration. Fill a clear drinking glass half full of water. Ask each child to tell you whether she thinks the glass is half full or half empty. After they respond, compare this to the way in which people look at the world around them. Some people have a positive attitude about life, always looking for the good side of things, and are grateful for the blessings they enjoy in life. They are the ones who usually see the glass as being half full. Other people have a more negative attitude, focusing on what they don't have in life, and they tend to see the glass as half empty. Ask the children which of these two types of people would generally be happier. What kind of attitude do you have? Are you a complainer or a complimenter? Can you change your attitude if you decide you want to?

13
The Heat Is On

Group size: 2 or more

Age: 5 and up

Materials: 2 pieces white paper; iron and ironing board; lemon juice or milk; pointed instrument like a toothpick, small paintbrush, hairpin, or pencil eraser

*T*his is an activity that amazes kids and is one that they'll want to show all their friends—it leaves a lasting impression! For it to be effective, you need to prepare the materials before you demonstrate it to the children.

You are going to create invisible words on the papers. Dip the point of a toothpick into the milk or lemon juice and with it, carefully write in big letters the words "I can" on one paper and "I can't" on the other. (For very young children, draw a simple happy face on one paper and a sad face on the other.) Let the liquid dry. You won't be able to see the words. Turn your iron on so it will be hot for the activity.

Now you're ready to begin. Show the two papers to the child and ask if she can see any difference between them. Tell her that the papers represent two people who are very different from each other, but that you can't really tell the difference from looking at them. The thing that sets these people apart is their attitude: one person is positive and has self-confidence, believing she can overcome most obstacles in life, and the other person is negative and pessimistic.

With younger children it's more effective to make up a story to go along with the demonstration. You might say something like, "This is Emily and this is Jackie. From the outside they look the same, but they are different on the inside. Emily believes almost anything is possible; she's happy and pleasant most of the time. Jackie is grouchy and whines a lot. She gets discouraged and doesn't think she's good at much of anything . . ." Continue the rest of the demonstration within the framework of the story.

Discuss the fact that our attitudes aren't overly apparent in some of our day-to-day activities: both optimists and pessimists (Emily and Jackie) can do well in school, can have close friends, can develop their talents, etc. Both kinds of people can get by in the world, although the ones with a positive attitude will be much happier and more fulfilled in life. But *all* of us, at some point in life, will face certain situations that will try our patience—inconveniences, hardships, and challenges that will weigh upon us and bring out our true nature. At this point, you should press the hot iron on one of the papers, keeping it pressed down for 15 to 20 seconds. Then repeat the process with the other paper.

As you show the two papers with their newly visible messages, tell the child that in the heat of our difficulties, our true attitude will manifest itself and be a determining factor in whether or not we can overcome the obstacles in our lives. Ask the child whether she can tell the difference between two people who have different attitudes. Does she have any friends, teachers, coaches, grandparents, or cousins who have a negative attitude? How does she feel about those people?

14
In and Out of Focus

Group size: 2 or more

Age: 6 and up

Materials: None

*T*his is another activity that can be done anywhere, anytime, and without any preparation. It can be adjusted to any location or situation.

Ask the child to look around and identify as many circular objects as she can find (buttons, the sun, a clock, shoelace eyelet, lamp shade, a ball, a dish, an orange, an eyeball, etc.). Or give a specific number—ask her to identify six things she can see that are round.

Now ask her to look around and find as many rectangle-shaped things as possible (a sign, a table, a wall, a TV, a building, a window, a candy bar, a block, a book). You can continue with this activity as long as you can keep the child's attention. Other categories to look for might include:

square things	black things
triangle-shaped things	moving things
green things	living things

After you have done several of these, ask the following questions:

• When you were looking for circles, did you notice a lot of rectangles?

• When you were looking for green things, did you see a lot of black things?

• When you were concentrating on finding living objects, did you count up how many nonliving objects you saw?

The answers to these questions will be "no" for most people. Now discuss the idea of "focus." We tend to see those things on which we are focused. If we are focused on circles, we'll find circles; if we are looking for triangles, our eyes and our minds will pick out triangles.

Discuss the fact that the same principle applies to our lives: if we are focused on our problems, the negative things in our lives, we will continue to see only those things. If we focus on our good qualities, our blessings and the things that bring us happiness, we will have a more positive outlook on life.

Ask how we can apply this same principle to the way in which we view our family and friends. Can you look for the good in people as well as the bad? Which will make you a happier person? What will focusing on the good in others do for you? What kind of person do people like to be around—one who sees the good in others or one who constantly talks about their faults?

PART FOUR

Honesty and Integrity

For the children:

Whitewashing the pump doesn't make it give pure water. That must come from down inside the well.

For the parents:

Moral is what you feel good after. Immoral is what you feel bad after.

—*Ernest Hemingway*

Kristen Wilson was hugging her seven-year-old son, Sam, and asking him how he did in school that day. "Great," he said.

"How about math?" she asked.

"Great!" was the quick reply.

"Did you get them all right? Did you have enough time to finish?"

"Yep."

"Okay—what's twelve take away five?"

Sam thought for a minute, then replied, "That's the *only* one I need to work on."

Well, you know what they say: "There will always be prayer in school as long as there are math tests!"

Teaching children honesty can be a challenge at the very least, given the epidemic proportions of dishonesty they see every day in the world around them. People lying to news reporters and stealing money from the government, students cheating on tests, friends sneaking into movies, and even their own parents breaking the speed limit or telling "convenient lies" over the phone.

While we can't control what children observe in the rest of the world, we *can* control what they see at home. If kids see the example of parents who are even occasionally dishonest, they soon learn the lesson that fibbing is the fastest way out of a sticky situation and an effective way to get what you want. Unfortunately, they also learn the lesson that parents can't always be trusted. Too often kids get mixed messages from their parents' reactions, as is reflected in the example of one distraught mother who said to her friend, "Are you troubled by the fact that your children occasionally tell lies?" To which her friend replied, "Not nearly as much as when they tell the truth at inappropriate times!"

Naturally, honesty takes on different meanings at various stages of development with children. There is a world of difference between a toddler who spills a glass of juice and then says, "I didn't do it" and a teenager who steals an expensive watch from a store and says, "I didn't take it." But generally, if we exemplify complete honesty in our homes, children will eventually learn the advantages of being trusted by others, of having an honest reputation, of taking responsibility for their own actions, and of being emotionally honest with others and with themselves.

When thinking about honesty and children, it's helpful to consider the various reasons kids tell lies from time to time. Not surprisingly, most of them are the same reasons adults tell lies. Kids lie to conceal guilt or avoid punishment: "I didn't take Susan's sweater! Stop blaming me for everything that goes wrong!" They lie to impress others or win acceptance: "My dad is the president of his company and makes tons of money, but he doesn't like to show off. That's why he drives an old car." They lie to avoid disapproval: "I turned that library book in last week. You must've lost it or given it out to someone else."

Sometimes kids lie to get someone else in trouble because of jealousy or competitiveness: "Mom, I saw David taking money out of your purse while you were on the phone." And occasionally, a child will lie as a deliberate hostile act in a parent-child struggle: "I have *not* been smoking cigarettes. You can't prove it so what are you going to do about it?" Kids seem to catch on very early that the "Pinocchio factor" only works in the movies—that their noses will *not* grow each time they tell a fib, and that sometimes compromising their honesty is much less painful than paying the consequences for their actions.

Children's consciences develop slowly and in relation to their age and general maturity level. But even with a developed conscience, kids still have to be repeatedly trained and taught about being honest and having personal integrity, and then taught the same lessons over and over again when they slip and fall short. And, of course, the best way to encourage honesty in our kids is to praise them profusely when they are honest. As parents, we need to be less anxious to "catch" our kids in a lie and more anxious to "catch" them telling the truth and praising them for it. The following activities will give you methods for discussing the important subjects of honesty and integrity in some creative and playful ways.

15

All Tied Up

Group size: 3 or more

Age: 3 and up

Materials: ball of yarn or string, a chair

*B*efore you begin this activity, *secretly arrange with one* member of your family to give a false answer to each question you ask her. This will only apply, however, after you ask her to sit in the chair in the center of the group. Start out by talking briefly about honesty. Ask your child or family members if they can think of an incident in their life when they made the decision to be honest, even when it might have been easier to be dishonest. Ask each one who shares something how it made her feel to be honest.

Now ask the designated person to sit in the chair. Start out by asking her a simple question such as, "Why were you so late coming home from school today?" As she answers with a lie, such as that she had to stay after school, wrap a long string of yarn around her once. Then ask her a follow-up question based on the first reply, such as, "Why did you have to stay after school?" As she makes up another answer, wrap the yarn around her once more. Continue to ask her follow-up questions regarding this same incident, wrapping the string around her each time she tells a lie. Eventually she will be tied to the chair, entangled in a web of yarn.

After the other children observe her in this tangled mess, explain that you asked this person to make up answers to all your questions—to lie. Then discuss some of the following ideas:

- Ask them if they can see what telling lies can do to someone. Emphasize how one lie usually leads to another and how quickly we can become trapped, embarrassed, or enslaved by lies.

- Ask them what will be experienced by the person who always tells the truth (not having to remember what his last lie was or how to cover it up, a clear conscience, peace of mind, and feeling good about himself).

- Ask the kids to tell about times when someone has been caught in a lie, or has had to tell a lie to cover up a prior one (they might even volunteer a personal experience).

- Ask why else it's important to always tell the truth (safety, trust, because it's right).

16
The Tower of Flour

Group size: 3 or more

Age: 3 and up

Materials: flour, dime, drinking glass (preferably plastic), dish towel or newspaper, dinner or butter knife, paper plate

*T*his is a fun game in and of itself, but it can also teach children ways in which outside influences affect their lives. Spread newspaper or a large dish towel on the kitchen table or counter. Place a dime in the center of the bottom of the drinking glass. Scoop flour into the glass, piling it to the brim and pressing it down firmly to make it compact. Place the paper plate on top of the glass and turn them over together on the dishtowel or newspaper. Tap the glass gently, and carefully lift it off. The flour will hopefully remain standing in the shape of the glass with the dime on top. If it doesn't, repeat the procedure, packing the flour more firmly, until it stands on its own.

First, play the game without any "moral" analogy—simply let everyone have the fun of participating. Each person takes a turn and, with a knife, carefully slices off an edge of the "flour tower," being careful not to cut too deeply. The object of the game is for the dime to stay on top of the tower and not fall down into it. As each person removes more and more of the flour, the tower becomes narrower and narrower, and the dime's position becomes increasingly precarious. The person whose slice causes the tower to cave in and the dime to drop is eliminated from the game, but he must first remove the fallen coin, using only his lips (or teeth, if necessary). Put the dime in the bottom and pack the glass with flour again. Play until there is only one player left.

On the next round, you should start by explaining that we can compare the tower of flour to our lives. Like the tower of flour, made up of small particles of flour, we are each made up of a lot of small things: our personalities, our experiences, our abilities, the inherited qualities from our parents, our feelings (simplify these things for young children). Throughout our childhood we are taught and molded by our parents, friends, and teachers (as the glass molds the flour). The coin at the top of the tower represents the best parts of our character or our "goodness"—the qualities of honesty and integrity we possess (again, simplify for small children).

Slicing away the tower represents the negative outside influences of the world and the ability they have to chip away at our integrity, to erode our strengths, and to slowly, imperceptibly eat away at our character (point out that there are many positive influences in the world but for now we are talking about the negative ones). Finally, if we allow these bad influences (the wrong friends, drinking, drugs, stealing, telling lies, cheating in school) to affect or control us, they will take their toll, causing the best in us to crumble and fall (the coin dropping). When that happens, it is often difficult to "come out on top" again unless we can find something or someone to help us rebuild and start over (filling the glass and beginning again).

During this part of the activity it is fun to have each player name a bad influence as they take their slice of flour. The child or player can simply say "lying" or "smoking a cigarette" or he can make up a little scenario like "today when Rachel's friends wanted to steal a candy bar from the store, Rachel made the decision to do it with them," or "Andy broke a window in a neighbor's house and didn't tell anyone he did it." Again, this can be adjusted according to the age group.

17

Now You See It, Now You Don't

Group Size: 2 or more

Age: 4 and up

Materials: 3 drinking glasses, water, chlorine bleach, food coloring (any color except yellow)

*B*efore you begin, fill two glasses about two thirds full of water. Fill the third glass about half full of chlorine bleach, but do it beforehand so no one sees what it is. Show the two glasses of water and tell everyone that they represent two friends. You can give them names of people in the group or assign them silly names.

For younger children, tell a story about the two friends, making it up as you go. For older children, you can also use a story, but make the examples more age-appropriate. I'll use the example of Patrick and Mike:

"For the most part, Patrick tries to obey his parents and generally does the right things, but Mike always seems to be getting into trouble. Patrick walks quickly to school, while Mike dawdles and throws rocks and sticks as he saunters through the neighborhood. One day Michael threw a rock and accidentally broke a house window. He ran on to school and never told anyone about it." Continue with the story, adding several more instances of Mike's lying to his parents, stealing a five-dollar bill, cheating on a test at school, etc.

As you relate the story, add one drop of food coloring to Mike's glass each time he does something wrong or dishonest. Don't stir it; just let it slowly dissipate in the water.

Point out that the first time Mike did something dishonest, the color didn't affect too much of the water, but each time he did something wrong, "he" became darker and cloudier, the "stain" finally permeating his entire being, filling him with guilt. Meanwhile, Patrick's glass remains clean and pure.

"Eventually, Mike felt miserable. His friends didn't want to be with him because he constantly got involved in dangerous and foolish activities. He soon felt entangled in all his lies and disliked himself more and more. After a serious talk with the school principal, he decided he needed to change his ways. First he went to the neighbor whose window he had broken, apologized, and offered to pay for the repair."

As you tell this part of the story, pour a little bleach (about a teaspoon) into Mike's glass. Keep adding to the story by relating examples of how Mike repented of his ways and started being more honest, repaying and apologizing to the people whom he had offended. With each honorable act, pour in a little bleach. Those watching will think you are just adding more water to Mike's glass, but they will be amazed as the colored water starts to fade. Eventually it will be almost completely clear.

This whole scenario can be adapted for older children and even teenagers and adults, just by making the story elements more appropriate to their age.

There are many things that can come out of this activity. It will lead to lots of questions and interesting discussion with small children, and can be extremely thought-provoking on a more sophisticated level. Here are a few ideas for discussion:

- If we had poured only one drop of color in the water (if Mike had been dishonest only once), how much bleach (his attempt to change for the good) would have been needed to clear it up? The sooner you clear up a lie or act of dishonesty, the better. The darker the water, the more drops of bleach (the more reparations and apologies) it takes to make it clear.

- How do the "Mike" and "Patrick" water glasses differ now? (Patrick's water is completely clear while Mike's is just slightly discolored.) What does that tell us about the effects of dishonesty in our lives?

- What about forgiveness? Should the people whom Mike offended forgive him? Will they be able to trust him from now on? What enables you to trust someone?

- How do you think Mike feels about himself now? Which way do you think he was happier? What's the difference between short-term happiness (being able to buy something with the 5 dollars he stole or getting a good grade on a test on which he cheated) and long-term happiness?

• What are the steps you need to go through to make amends for an act of dishonesty? (1) Recognize you've done something wrong; (2) repair the relationship—apologize to the person you offended; (3) restore what you have damaged; (4) resolve not to do it again.

18

Shape Up!

Group size: 2 or more

Age: 5 and up

Materials: 1 cup cornstarch, ½ cup water, bowl,
food coloring (optional)

This is a simple activity that applies more to one's general character and integrity than merely to honesty. First, mix together 1 cup cornstarch with ½ cup water in a bowl. Stir the mixture with a spatula or spoon. You can add a few drops of food coloring just for fun, if you desire. This "recipe" is a little tricky, and it's important to have it just the right consistency. It should be thick enough to hold together as a "glob," but fluid enough to droop and drip when you hold it still. You may have to add a few drops of water at a time until you get it right, as you knead it in your hands. It would be best to get the consistency right before you start the activity.

To begin, talk about the word "integrity." Explain that the word means the state of being whole or complete. It means to be upright and in perfect condition. It also means being completely honest. Now, pick up the glob you have made and start talking about it as if it were a child—more specifically, one of the children present. As you mold it into a ball with both hands, talk about the things in the child's life that mold his character, the things that will turn him into a productive, happy, and well-rounded person. Talk about the qualities that will eventually shape his personality and form his value system. Explain that having integrity is one quality that will keep him whole, complete, well rounded, and happy. As you talk about these things, keep patting the ball with your hands to keep its shape round and uniform.

Some examples of how a child can show integrity in his daily life are studying hard in school and doing homework assignments, being loyal and dependable to family and friends, avoiding the temptation to lie or cheat, being fair and honest in his sports activities, and obeying his parents and teachers.

This demonstration can be applied to one particular area of the child's life (demonstrating integrity at school, integrity with family members, with his basketball team), or it can apply to the development of good character in general. It can easily be individualized for the age and particular strengths and/or weaknesses of each child.

At some point during this activity, stop patting the ball with your hands and hold it still in one hand with the palm facing up and your fingers slightly spread apart. When you do this, tell the child there will be times in life when we might let down our guard, relax our standards, get tired, or for some other reason weaken and make some wrong choices.

As you continue to hold the cornstarch ball still, explain that if we allow these weaknesses to become habits and let them develop unchecked over a period of time, they can have a negative effect on our individual growth and cause our "well-rounded" character to sink, slump, and droop. By this point, the cornstarch ball will have lost its shape and be oozing out through your fingers, sagging and dripping down to create a mess below. You can ask questions about why it takes continual work, attention, focus, and "muscle" to maintain one's integrity when faced with temptations and obstacles.

Part Five

Love and Kindness

For the children:

It's nice to be important, but it's more important to be nice.

For the parents:

If love isn't taught in the home, it is almost impossible to learn anywhere else.

Dear God,

I bet it is very hard for you to love all of everybody in the whole world. There are only four people in our family and I can never do it.

—Larry

P.S. Maybe brothers like Cain and Abel would not kill each other so much if they had their own rooms. It works with my brother.

Recently our family was returning from a day in San Francisco. We approached the bridge where a dollar toll is required and we dutifully paid the man in the booth our dollar. Then, quite unexpectedly, my teenage son Seth quickly took a dollar bill from his pocket, handed it to the man, and said, "This is for the car in back of us!" The man was as surprised as we were, but he gave Seth a pleased wink and we were on our way. Naturally, we all glanced out the back window to see the reaction of the people in the next car as the man in the toll booth declined their payment and explained that it was "on us."

Our son had performed a seemingly insignificant "random act of kindness," but it had caused all of us to laugh with delight just to think about how the total strangers in the next car might be feeling. For some reason, I thought about this experience the whole way home, and less than a half hour later, as I tried to referee two younger children fighting over a game, one thing became disturbingly clear to me: sometimes it's easier to show kindness toward total strangers, friends, or acquaintances than to the members of our own family.

Living together day after day, seeing each other at our best and our worst, creates an environment that is not always conducive to loving responses from brothers and sisters or husbands and wives.

It has been said that if love isn't taught in the home, it is almost impossible to learn anywhere else. But any parent knows that love doesn't always come naturally to children, and kind words and actions need to be taught and practiced within a family setting. If someone wants to be a good baseball player, he practices pitching, catching, and batting for hundreds of hours to improve and master his skills. Although we don't think of kindness and love as "skills," there are ways to practice with children the types of responses that will promote love, empathy, patience, and courtesy within the home.

Rabbi Steven Carr Reuben reminds us that we need to teach our children "that greatness lies not in the splashy headlines of life, but in the small print—not just in coming through in the rare moments of extraordinary crisis, but in being there for others in the simple, ordinary moments of their everyday lives." The home is the ideal setting to teach and encourage such behavior in children, with parents repeatedly pointing out examples of kind acts, and praising their children for those as much as they praise them for bringing home good grades in science or math.

One mother told me about the time she was getting ready to deliver her third child. Her three-year-old son, Peter, was excited as they talked about having a new baby at home, but her six-year-old daughter, Katie, was displaying signs of resentment and jealousy toward the upcoming "competition." When a darling baby girl named Sydney came home from the hospital with Mom and Dad, Katie started sulking and sucking her thumb. She ignored Sydney as much as possible but would secretly pinch her and make her cry when she thought her parents weren't looking. Although this is not an unusual response for an older sibling, especially one of the same sex as the new baby, Katie's mother was concerned and wanted to find ways to make Katie feel as important and loved as the new baby. She began by gathering her whole family around and conducted the activity called Light My Fire.

19

Light My Fire

Group size: 3 or more

Age: 2 and up

Materials: 1 candle for each family member, matches, newspaper

---

*P*ass out candles to each member of the family; six-to-eight-inch tapered candles are best, but other kinds will work. Do this activity in the kitchen over the table or counter. Put newspapers down to catch any dripping wax. Turn off most of the lights in the area so the candlelight will be more discernible. Obviously, caution should be taken for the safety of small children (a parent or older sibling can place her hand around the child's hand holding the candle).

A parent should light his or her candle first. Tell the children that the flame represents love. Now light your spouse's candle with your burning candle and talk about how you decided to get married and share your love together. If there is no spouse, simply light the old-est child's candle instead.

Now, with your candle, continue to light each of the children's candles in order of their birth. You can talk about the love you felt as each child came into your family. As you light each one, hold your wick next to his wick and watch how the flame intensifies momentarily as it is lighting the next candle. When everyone's candle is lit, ask different family members some of the following questions, which might help your children begin to share their feelings about expressing love and kindness within your family:

- "As I passed my light to each of you, did my light get any smaller? [No.] By giving my love away to each additional child, is any love taken away from the original child or the spouse? [No.] When love is divided among members of a large family, is there less love for each? [No.]"

- "Is there more or less light in the room with everyone's candle lit than when just mine is burning? [More.] Do we have enough light as a family to share it with those around us who seem sad or lonely? What are some ways we can share our light as a family, and who are the people who might need some of our light? Will our light diminish as we share it with others outside our family circle?"

- "What happens when we all hold our candles together and make our flames touch each other's? Do you see how our light burns brighter together as a family than it does for each individual alone?"

This activity didn't solve all of Katie's problems, but her mother reported that Katie was really impressed by the fact that after her baby sister's candle (held by her father) had been lit by her mother, Katie's flame still burned "as big as it did before." Her attitude toward baby Sydney seemed to soften a little after this candlelight class on family love.

As I did this activity with my family, the children seemed to grasp the idea immediately. They also had other insights I had never considered. That's one of the intriguing aspects of playing these games: your children will surprise you with their irresistibly fresh perspective on things and, as always, you'll probably learn just as much from them as they do from you.

My oldest son, Ryan, made the comment that as one candle lights another, the temporary increase in the flame might be compared to the love parents feel the minute a new baby is born. For a while it might seem like all their attention is focused on the baby and that the other children are less important. However, just as the flames subside and equal out, eventually all family members should, hopefully, feel equally loved. This was an interesting comment from Ryan, as he enjoyed being the "only child" for the first few years of his life, and had a relatively tough time when, at age two, he felt uprooted by a new baby brother. I think Ryan understands now that each child in our family is very special and loved in very individual ways.

As I asked some of the above questions, my daughter Kelly, eight years old at the time, came up with a lesson I won't forget. She said, "Mom, if there's someone in the family whose light goes out for a while, it can be lit again by any one of the people around him whose light is still burning." She was perceptive enough to know that most families will experience times when a certain member, for whatever reason, will struggle with keeping a "bright light." Depending on the situation, that person might receive the love and encouragement he needs from a wise parent, a sympathetic older sister, a trusted grandparent, or even the unconditional adoration of a nine-month-old baby brother. I suspect Kelly also recognized that sometimes it might even be one of the parents' lights that grows dim. What a gift it is to have family around you who are sensitive and eager, or at least willing, to rekindle your flame during those dark times!

20

A Spoonful of Sugar

Group size: 2 or more

Age: 4 and up

Materials: bowl of water, pepper, sugar, bar of soap

Sprinkle pepper liberally on the water. Tell the child that the pepper represents the people around her—her friends, brothers and sisters, parents and teachers. You can name names and talk about how she interacts with those people in real life. Discuss the fact that how we get along with those people is largely determined by how we treat them and speak to them. Words can be very powerful tools, either for good or bad, and it's important to learn positive and kind ways of speaking to our friends. If the child is old enough, talk with her about the meaning of the saying, "Sticks and stones will break my bones, but words will break my heart."

Now talk about an example of someone who does not use kind words when speaking to others. Tell the child that the bar of soap represents negative, harsh language. Have the child touch the soap to the center of the water. The soap will repel the pepper and will cause it to be dispersed to the sides of the bowl. Make the comparison that when we speak unkindly to others, they won't want to be around us, and will want to scatter.

Take a teaspoon of sugar and pour it in the center of the water, comparing the sugar to the sweetness of kind and thoughtful words. The pepper will be drawn into the sugar. Talk about how being loving toward other people usually causes them to be drawn to us, and makes them want to be our friends.

21
The Love Eggs-periment

Group size: 2 or more

Age: 4 and up

Materials: clear drinking glass filled with 1 cup water, 1 fresh egg, ¼ cup salt, tablespoon, permanent marker

*F*or young children, draw a face on one side of the egg (this is optional for older children). Carefully place the egg in the glass of water and observe that it sinks to the bottom. Tell the children that the egg represents someone who is not receiving love or acceptance from those around him. Sinking to the bottom represents how someone who is ridiculed or made fun of would feel— low, sad, depressed, unappreciated.

Remove the egg from the water and set it aside. One tablespoon at a time, add the salt to the water. As you stir in each spoonful, explain that the salt represents different ways to make someone feel loved and accepted. You should try to use examples that are relevant to your child's life, such as offering to eat lunch with a new child at school, bringing cookies to a new family in the neighborhood, helping someone who has fallen off her bike, sharing a special toy with a friend, etc. After you have added all the salt, replace the egg to show how it is now supported with "love" and "held up" by the encouragement and acceptance of others.

This demonstration can be centered around showing love and support within the family, in a school classroom or extracurricular team, or within a religious or community group or organization.

22
Spin the Bottle

Group size: 4 or more

Age: 3 and up

Materials: soda bottle, paper, pencil, bowl or other container

---

*B*efore you play this game, write down on about 20 slips of paper some of the instructions listed below, or make up your own. You can write the same item two or three times. Fold the papers and put them in the bowl.

- Give someone in the circle a hug.

- Tell about something helpful that someone in the circle did for you lately.

- Say something you like about someone in the group.

- Promise to do a small good deed for someone tomorrow.

- Name a talent possessed by someone in the group.

- Tell about a time when you observed someone in the group showing love for someone else.

Sit in a circle and lay the soda bottle in the middle of the circle. Have the appointed person spin the bottle.

After the bottle stops spinning, have the person the bottle points to pick a slip of paper from the container. The person must do what the paper instructs. After he or she has complied with the instruction, the paper is thrown out and that person then spins the bottle to determine who will have the next turn.

A simplified version of this game is to do it without any written instructions. You simply spin the bottle, and everyone in the circle has to say something positive about the person the bottle is pointing to, such as a talent, something the person has improved in, etc.

PART SIX

Developing Habits

For the children:

> Do it.
> Do it right.
> Do it right now.

For the parents:

What should not be heard by little ears should not be
spoken by big mouths.

Six-year-old Gray was explaining to his parents about the small fire that had taken place at school that day: "I knew it was going to happen," he said, "because we've been practicing for it all year!"

Teachers, like parents, know that if children practice something over and over, it will soon become a habit, a pattern they fall into naturally without much thought or effort. Adults also understand that the earlier these positive habits are ingrained, the better. Aristotle articulated this principle when he said, "Good habits formed at youth make all the difference." Although establishing habits isn't actually a value in itself, its impact for good or bad is so powerful, it's imperative that parents give guidance in this area.

Bad habits are just as easy for kids to develop as good habits, and may actually have a stronger hold on them because in many cases the immediate physical or psychological benefit derived from the habit seems many times greater than its negative impact. Children can be taught, however, that although there may be a period of struggle in breaking a bad habit, the struggle will be followed by a sense of freedom when the new pattern becomes a good habit. They will eventually understand the principle that good habits might be difficult to acquire but are easy to live with; bad habits are easy to acquire but difficult to live with.

When a person chooses a habit, he also chooses the end result. And those results can have far-reaching consequences. I remember the story of a mother who went into her son's bedroom and said, "Come on now, it's time to get up. It's time to go to school." Her son pulled the covers over his head and groaned, "I won't. . . . I won't go. . . . I hate school!" The mother replied, "You have to go, it's important." He stuck his head out from under the covers again and said, "Yeah? Just give me two good reasons for going to school." And his mother replied, "First, you're forty-two years old. Second, you're the principal." Parents can determine much about their children's future just by helping them develop good habits in their early years!

Habits, good and bad, end up affecting most areas of life. At my house, some of the habits displayed at the dinner table make me wonder whether I've taught my kids anything. Yes, there are elbows on the table, boardinghouse reaches for the butter, napkins ending up everywhere but in a lap, and more than occasional slurps and burps (I have five children—all girls except *four*!). Even an inquiry as to whether this is how they'd act if they were dining at the White House or on their first date doesn't seem to faze them, and I sometimes feel like throwing in the towel and giving up completely on the idea of raising well-mannered children.

But just when I start chanting to myself through clenched teeth, "Lower your expectations, lower your expectations, lower . . ." one of them dashes off with his basketball and yells back, "Hey, Mom . . . good dinner!" and my hardened parental heart turns into a helpless pool of sentimental slush. Trying to instill good habits in your children is absolutely worth the effort, but not in a way that sacrifices happy, loving relationships.

The following activities are some painless ways to impress on your kids the importance of developing good habits.

23

Hanging by a Thread

Group size: 2 or more

Age: 4 and up

Materials: 2 sticks (popsicle sticks or small twigs), sewing thread

*H*ave a child hold two sticks in front of her about a foot apart, or have two children each hold a stick so that the sticks are about one foot apart. Wind the thread around the sticks one time and tie it. Ask the child holding the sticks to break the thread by pulling the sticks apart. Now wind the thread around the sticks two or three times and ask the child to break it. Add several more rounds of thread until it cannot be broken by pulling the sticks apart.

Explain that habits are like the thread. Bad habits (leaving toys out, not doing homework, not doing chores, talking back, smoking) are easy to break if caught in the beginning stages but become harder and harder to break the more we repeat them. On the other

hand, good habits (wearing your seat belt, brushing your teeth, making your bed, putting toys and clothes away, telling the truth) are strengthened each time they are practiced and can be encouraged and developed through repeated use. Eventually they will become so ingrained, they won't fade easily; like the thread wrapped around the sticks repeatedly, they will be strong.

Here are a few ideas for initiating discussion of developing and changing habits:

- What is an example of one good habit you think you have developed? Can you remember how it first became a habit?

- Do you know someone who has developed some bad habits? Do you think the person can break them? How?

- Are there any bad habits you might have developed that we should work on?

- Make a list of habits that need to be improved by the whole family, discuss them, and plan to work on one each month.

A father of four children, Chris Langford, told me of an experience he had with the above activity. He and his wife were concerned about their 12-year-old son, Matt, and the habit he seemed to be developing of using foul language. Matt was more careful around the house, but his parents overheard him several times talking to his friends, and his parents wanted to talk to him about the importance of breaking this bad habit before it became a way of life for him. With all four of their children, they conducted the sticks and string activity. Then, because this seemed a little elementary for Matt, Chris took him outside to reinforce the point they were trying to make.

As Matt and his father walked through a field in back of their house, Chris asked Matt to pull a small weed. Matt, anxious to do anything but have a serious father-son talk with his dad, pulled it up without any problem and tossed it aside. Every few minutes, Chris continued to ask his son to pull another weed, each time choosing a larger and larger one. As they walked, Chris broached the subject of the language he had noticed Matt using and how easily those things can develop into bad habits. Then he compared the habits to the weeds.

When weeds first sprout and are young, they are very easy to pluck up and wipe out; however, the longer you let them grow, the harder they are to uproot.

The last weed that his dad pointed to reached Matt's waist, and although he used all his strength, he wasn't able to pull it up. The point was obvious: just like the progression from new, manageable weeds to large, stubborn ones, the chains of habit are too weak to be felt until they are too strong to be broken.

Matt didn't say much during this time with his dad, but Chris felt that he had made his point without a long lecture, and was able to laugh and joke with Matt on the way into the house about the weeding that needed to be done in his *own* backyard.

24

May the Force Be with You

Group size: 2 or more

Age: 6 and up

Materials: 12-inch ruler, 1 sheet newspaper, table, marker

Before you begin, unfold a single sheet of newspaper and write the phrase "bad habits" in large letters across it. Talk about how people develop habits, both good and bad, and list some bad habits that might be typical of children their age. These could include things like whining, not obeying their parents, not wearing a seat belt, talking back, not brushing their teeth, using swear words, not doing chores, neglecting to wear a bike helmet, smoking cigarettes, using drugs, lying to friends and teachers, cheating on tests, etc. Again, if appropriate, you can concentrate on one particular problem the child might be having.

Place a ruler at the edge of a table and let it stick out about five inches. Explain that the ruler represents a person, or one of the children observing. Lay the newspaper over the section of the ruler that is on

the table. Ask if the children think these bad habits (the newspaper) are strong enough to hold the person (the ruler) down when you strike the free end of the ruler. They will undoubtedly respond that the newspaper is very flimsy and couldn't really restrict the ruler's movement in any way. Now sharply strike the free end of the ruler with your fist. The ruler should resist your blow or even break in half without causing the newspaper to tear. (This is caused by the amount of air pressure on such a relatively large piece of paper.)

Talk about the fact that bad habits can be deceiving, just as the flimsy newspaper is deceiving. People don't usually recognize the control that bad habits have over their lives, and the ability that such habits have to restrict their freedom. In many cases, it is more common for a bad habit to "break" the person than it is for the person to break the habit. Use the example of smoking cigarettes, and how the first cigarette seems to be innocent. Every smoker believes he will be strong enough to resist the next cigarette. Eventually, however, the accumulated effect of many cigarettes, like the large sheet of paper, causes so much pressure on the body to inhale nicotine that the person becomes a slave to the habit. They lose control over their own bodies.

With a younger child, talk about the habit of not brushing his teeth. The habit is deceptive at first; no child believes that going one night without brushing his teeth will have long-lasting effects. And it won't. But the accumulated effect over months or years of that bad habit may very well cause pain, expense, and an unsightly appearance.

25

All Change Hands

Group size: 2 or more

Age: 5 and up

Materials: None

---

*T*his is an extremely simple activity—one that can be done while riding in a car or trying to kill time in an airport or at the doctor's office. It can be done with one child or several at the same time.

- Ask the child to fold his hands together with fingers interlocking. Note which thumb is on top of the other. Now ask him to try to fold his hands with the other thumb on top, which will cause all his other fingers to shift their interlocking position. Ask if this new way feels comfortable.

- Ask the child to cross his legs at the knee. Note which leg is on top. Now ask him to cross his legs with the other on top. Ask if this feels comfortable.

- Ask the child to pretend he is in school and raising his hand to answer a question. Note which hand he raises. Is it the same hand he writes with? Is it the same hand whose thumb was on top when he folded his hands?

- Ask the child to fold his arms in front of his chest. Note which arm is on top of the other. Ask him if he can switch his arms and fold them with the opposite arm on top. This will be fairly difficult for most children (and adults) and you may have to help him. Ask if this feels comfortable.

- Ask the child to snap his fingers. Note which finger he uses to snap together with his thumb. Ask him to try snapping with his index, third, or fourth finger instead and ask him if it feels natural.

- Ask the child to clap his hands together several times. One hand will usually be slightly on top of the other. Ask him to switch and clap with the other hand on top.

Explain how difficult it is to undo a habit once it is ingrained. In none of the above examples is there a right or wrong way of doing the action. Each individual develops his own way of snapping and clapping at a fairly young age, and then continues to respond the same way his entire life once the pattern has been set.

Discuss the fact that with some habits, however, there *is* a right or wrong way to respond (being on time or being late, exercising or being lazy), and many of those habits have serious far-reaching consequences. It's important to develop smart habits from the very beginning.

26

The "No" Game

Group size: 4 or more

Age: 5 and up

Materials: a dollar bill for each person, ribbon or string, safety pins

*T*his is a great game for many different types of groups and occasions. It can be played by a small family sitting around the dinner table or it can be used as an ice-breaker for a large group of adults or teens. The only catch is that you need some cash to play it.

Cut and tie a piece of ribbon or string long enough to fit comfortably over each person's head, like a long necklace. Safety-pin a dollar bill onto the bottom of each ribbon, so each person is "wearing" a dollar. If you want to be very extravagant, for a special party or "Olympic game night," get silver dollars and tape them to the ribbons. For a large gathering when you don't want to fork out a dollar for each participant, simply ask all the guests for a dollar bill as they arrive and tell them they might be able to double or triple it in a half hour.

This game is particularly good for the beginning of a party, to get people mixing and talking to each other. It demonstrates that many of the words and expressions we use in speaking to other people—our automatic responses—come about as a result of habit.

Set a timer for 15 minutes or a half hour, whichever you feel is appropriate. Explain that if anyone hears someone saying the words "no" or "know" during the set time period, they can take the dollar necklace from that person and put it around their own neck, adding to their dollar. If Will has collected five dollars around his neck and Brooke hears him say "no," Brooke takes all five dollars. It doesn't matter how many bills you have around your neck—if someone catches you saying "no" you must give up the whole bunch.

When the timer goes off and the game is over, everyone gets to keep what they are "wearing" at that moment. I have seen people leave a party $30 richer than when they arrived. This is a very effective way to get people mingling, and it usually gets very intense and funny, as everyone focuses on trying to illicit a "no" or "I don't know" response from anyone who consents to talk to them.

Obviously, this game can be played just for fun. It's one of my family's favorites and we've done it over the years with many different-size groups. However, it can also be used to introduce the subject of the power of our habits. Even with a monetary incentive to avoid saying one small word, it is very difficult to overcome our ingrained responses. This activity can kick off a discussion about how we communicate with each other and how that communication might be improved.

Ask your children what their automatic responses might be to the following situations; then ask them to think about other, more effective ways to respond. Make up other situations appropriate for your children's ages.

- A really mean boy at school kicks a ball hard and it lands right in your face.

- Your sister borrows your sweater and you find it in a dirty heap on the floor.

- You're playing an exciting computer game and your dad calls you outside to mow the lawn.

- You have just gotten glasses and an older kid at school calls you "four eyes."

- At your birthday party, all the kids start playing with the toys you just received as gifts.

To find satisfaction in relationships, children need to learn a multitude of social skills; effective communication is one of the most important. Because kids are vigilant observers, and are always learning from what they see and hear, parents need to set the tone for positive, effective, and respectful speaking and listening in the home. The communication habits children develop in the family setting can hinder them in later life, or help them conquer the world.

PART SEVEN

Goal Setting

For the children:

Yard by yard, it's so hard! Inch by inch, it's a cinch!

For the parents:

If you're going to leave footprints in the sands of time, you'd better wear your working shoes.

—*LeGrande Richards*

When my youngest son came home from his first day in kindergarten, I asked him if he had learned very much that day. He replied, "Nah, I gotta go back again tomorrow." He would soon learn that most of life is a series of "going-back-agains"— learning things little by little, one step at a time. Most children are familiar with the Olympics, and have seen the success of very young athletes whose goal it is to win the gold. What some kids might not understand is that the Olympians who reach that level have probably been taking small steps over a long period of time, setting their feet on each rung on their ladder to success by setting attainable goals, which, along with hard work, has allowed them to realize their dreams.

Not all our kids will go to the Olympics, but all children have needs and wants, hopes and dreams, things they want to accomplish—especially as they get older. It's a good idea to start talking about setting small, reachable goals when your children are fairly young, and to find ways to help them feel good about their accomplishments.

Now, for some of us, even the mention of the word "goal" triggers the gag reflex, because we have set so many goals in our lives and then failed to accomplish such a large percentage of them. How many times have we resolved to lose 20 pounds and then given up on the third day (or third hour)? Or how about that vegetable garden we were going to plant that instead ended up being two potted marigolds? And what about those classes we were going to take at night to get our career on track? After working all day and coming home to the kids' baseball, dancing, chicken pox, and science projects, we drop into bed, almost relieved that our checking account was too overdrawn that week to pay the class fee.

As frazzled parents entering a new millennium in overdrive, we can usually chalk off *yesterday* to experience and regard *tomorrow* with hope—but *today* is simply an attempt to survive getting from one to the other! How can we talk to our kids about the importance of setting goals when it seems like such a futile exercise in our own hectic lives?

The answer is that the frenzied pace of modern life makes establishing goals that much more imperative. Setting goals is to time what establishing a budget is to money. We can show our kids that goals, like a budget, teach us to sacrifice an immediate reward for a more satisfying future one. Even failed goals nudge us in the right direction. If we don't quite make it this time, we set more realistic expectations and go for it again. As our kids observe us sometimes succeeding and sometimes failing, they'll learn that it's okay to bump our heads and stub our toes occasionally, to be less than perfect.

They will also come to understand that making mistakes in life usually provides remarkable opportunities to learn. As they watch us "pick ourselves up, dust ourselves off, and start all over again," our children will begin to feel a sense of their own personal resilience. No one needs to earn a black belt in goal setting; we only need to learn how to take the baby steps that will eventually lead us toward our dreams and ideals. Try some of the following activities to help your kids start thinking about their own goals.

27
Goalies

Group size: 2 or more

Age: 5 and up

Materials: handful of pennies or other coins

---

*E*xplain to a child that you're going to play a little game. Show her the handful of pennies and tell her that these are special pennies called "goalies." Stand a few feet away from the child and ask her to see if she can catch the "goalies" when you toss them. Then toss seven or eight or the whole handful of coins in one throw. Naturally, they will go all over the place and your child will probably catch only one or two, if any.

Now try it again, except this time, carefully toss just one coin at a time to the child. After you have gone through all the coins, count how many she was able to catch (hopefully, most of them).

Explain that the reason these pennies are called "goalies" is that they are like goals. When we try to work on too many goals at the same time, it is difficult, and most of the goals won't be accomplished—like the pennies tossed all at once, most of which will be caught. But when we take each goal one or two at a time, with planning and forethought, we will have more success and less tendency to feel overwhelmed.

For older children and teenagers this activity can also relate to the principle of setting short-term and long-term goals. Just as the child was not able to catch all the pennies at one time, a long-term goal cannot be accomplished overnight. It needs to be broken down into smaller bites and taken one step at a time. This idea can be applied to such goals as learning to play the piano, earning scouting awards, working on a term paper or project for school, getting in shape, or saving money for a new bike, CD player, or college.

With young children, I usually extend this activity with a fun coin-toss game. The easiest way is to simply pitch pennies into a jar or bowl; each child is given three pennies and must stand behind a line or marker as he tosses his pennies. He gets a point for each penny that goes into the bowl. Then it's the next person's turn. A more challenging game is to toss coins into a muffin tin. You can count one point for every coin that lands in a cup, and two points for those landing in one of the two center cups. If you feel an enormous spurt of energy, you can put a small piece of masking tape inside each cup of the muffin tin and label each cup with a number (1 to 12 for a 12-cup muffin tin). Add up the total points from all the cups where a coin lands.

This activity worked for me with my son Alex when he was eight years old. One night as we talked, I could see his lip begin to tremble and his big blue eyes widen like saucers to hold his tears. He had just joined the Cub

Scouts and was very excited but also a little nervous about earning his first big advancement, his "Bobcat" badge. There was a page-long list of tasks required to achieve that rank, and he was feeling as though he ought to be able to accomplish them all in one night to "catch up" with the other kids in the troop. As I saw his frustration building, I grabbed a handful of pennies and played the above game.

I explained that just as he couldn't catch all the pennies at once, he wouldn't be able to do all his scouting requirements in one sitting. If he would tackle his goal of becoming a "Bobcat" one small step at a time, like catching one penny at a time, he would have much more success and feel less stressed. Alex understood the concept immediately, relaxed considerably, and we happily moved on to our muffin tin toss, problem solved!

28
Domino Dash

Group size: 2 or more

Age: 6 and up

Materials: 1 or more sets of dominoes

*L*ine up 30 dominoes standing on end in three rows of about 10 each, so that knocking the first one down will cause a chain reaction and knock down the whole row.

- The first row should have a small gap of two to three inches in the middle of the line so that the whole row will not fall down.

- The second row should have one domino in the middle of the row slightly off center, to keep a chain reaction from being completed.

- The third row should be straight, with all the dominoes close enough to ensure the successive fall of all of them.

Begin by explaining how setting goals can help you in life. This can be applied to getting good grades in school, completing a certain project, learning how to play the piano or baseball, doing chores, etc. Explain that in order to achieve a long-range goal, we must have several small, well-planned goals to keep us on course toward our ultimate goal. Each domino represents a small, well-planned step.

1. Have your child knock down the row with the gap. The dominoes will stop falling at the midpoint because of the gap. Point out that if we skip a vital step in our progression toward our main goal, we probably won't succeed. For example, if the child wants to earn money to buy a bike and mows lawns all summer as small steps to the larger goal, but then spends all the money on junk instead of putting it into savings, he is skipping a vital step in the plan, namely, saving all the money.

2. Have your child knock down the second row, the one with the off-center domino. Again, the chain reaction will be stopped in the middle.

Discuss the fact that if we don't stay on course with our goals, we won't achieve the desired result. For example, a child may join the school band to learn how to play the flute, but when it turns out to be more difficult than she thought, she gets sidetracked with her friend's electric keyboard and quits practicing the flute.

3. Have your child knock down the third row; the chain reaction will continue all the way to the end of the row. Talk about how small, well-planned goals will lead to success.

This activity will be more meaningful if you actually choose a goal that the child might be working on (running for office at school, saving to buy new shoes, memorizing a musical piece, completing a science project, etc.) and talk about some of the smaller short-term goals that would help him reach the long-term goal. You might point to each domino that represents each of the small goals. This fun activity might lead to some further discussion about the value of goal setting:

- Is it a good idea to write down your goals? Why? (It helps us define them, remember them, and commit to them.) For younger children, drawing pictures of goals can be just as effective.

- What can we do if we fail to reach our goal? (Don't get discouraged. . . . If at first you don't succeed, try, try again. . . . Making mistakes helps us learn and grow. . . . How can we do it differently next time?).

- Would life be more fun if we never tried to get better at anything? (It may seem easier now, but we'd be bored later on.)

Continue playing by making different patterns with the dominoes to see if you can knock them all down. Kids always think this is great fun, especially because they are usually better at it than Mom or Dad! Have contests to see who can knock down the longest string in one turn.

29
It's in the Mail

Group size: 2 or more

Age: 5 and up

Materials: paper, pen or pencil, envelope, postage stamp

*L*ay the paper, pen or pencil, envelope, and stamp out on a table. Talk briefly about setting goals and ask the child if she can think of one specific goal she'd like to work on in the next few weeks. For a young child this could be something like picking up her toys every day before dinner or learning to make her bed; for an older child, you might want to ask her to list several things she'd like to accomplish, like memorizing a poem for her class, learning to cook dinner, etc. Discuss the fact that unless we think about ways we want to make improvements in our lives, we won't progress and grow.

Explain to the child that the paper represents the thing that we want to accomplish. Ask the child to fold the paper, put it in the envelope, and seal it. The blank envelope is much like us until we have made a plan to reach our goals. Ask her where this blank envelope would go if she put it in the mailbox without an address on it. Even though we have thought about things we want to accomplish (the paper inside the envelope), until we actually decide *how* to make them happen, they have no direction (the blank envelope).

Have the child address the envelope, or for a small child, show him how you address it. It can be addressed to himself, or for fun, he can address it to a grandparent or friend. Emphasize that in this way, you are giving instructions to the mailman as to the direction it should go. Discuss what it means to give your goals direction (setting small, short-term goals to reach a larger goal; deciding a time by which you want to complete the goal; etc.).

Ask the child if the addressed envelope would reach its destination if you mailed it as is. Then have the child put the stamp on the letter and remind him that the stamp costs money. Compare the stamp to the price we have to pay to reach our goals. The price we pay might be things like sacrificing our time to work toward our goal, giving up fun activities to devote energy to the pursuit, the willingness to practice something over and over until we get proficient at it, or saving our money to buy the necessary tools, lessons, or equipment to accomplish our goal.

Only when the letter is written, the envelope addressed and stamped, can it reach its destination. In the same way, it is only when we think about our goals, write them down, determine how and when we will work on them, and pay the price required, that we will be able to accomplish those goals.

30

Knockout

Group size: 1 or more

Age: 5–10 years

Materials: empty cardboard boxes (like shoe boxes or tissue boxes), markers, colored paper or stickers

---

*T*his activity, like many in the book, can be used to explore the general principle of the section (goal setting, in this instance) with a whole family or a group of children, or it can be used to address a specific problem one child is having. The Knockout game is described here as played with one child, but it can be adapted to a larger group of children and a more general discussion.

First, help your child identify a goal she would like to achieve (learning to swim, sleeping in her own bed, saving money for a new computer game). Write the goal on a sticker or piece of paper and stick it to a wall. Next, discuss the things that are preventing her from attaining that goal, the obstacles she sees and her reasons for hesitation in moving forward (fear, monsters, temptation to spend money on junk, etc.). Write these obstacles on labels and stick them on the various boxes. Let the child stack the boxes to form a wall between herself and her goal.

Now, discuss the child's special skills that will help her overcome her stumbling blocks. These can be things like her creativity and optimism, or her having a good memory or being a good problem-solver, a good organizer, a quick learner, etc. As you talk, write each of those qualities on a sticker and affix it directly to the child. Another way to do this is to stick these "skill stickers" onto a pillow.

Talk about the fact that equipped with these special skills and unique characteristics, your child can accomplish almost anything she sets her mind to. Tell her to face the barricade and, with all her strength, to break through. Encourage her to really let loose and smash, demolish, and pulverize her obstacles (with her arms and legs or with the pillow). This activity may sound rowdy, but the uproarious fun can really give the child a sense of what it feels like to take action in accomplishing her goals.

PART EIGHT

Unity and Cooperation

For the children:

People are lonely because they build walls instead of bridges.

—*Joseph Newton*

For the parents:

The only time we fail in the home is when we give up on each other.

—*Marvin J. Ashton*

Okay, so you're not the Waltons—not too many families are these days. But once in a while it might be comforting to crawl into that Norman Rockwell painting and feel the coziness and warmth of an earlier era's family life. Unlike families of past generations, whose members relied heavily on one another for companionship, safety, and survival, many families today are hard-pressed to identify anything they share together other than their colds and their toothpaste.

In our fast-paced world, where cable TV, the Internet, sports, and an endless list of outside activities compete for our attention, family members may actually feel isolated from one another. Children naturally thrive on their parents' love and acceptance, but it's also important for them to feel the security that comes from the support of other relatives—brothers and sisters and extended family such as cousins, grandparents, and aunts and uncles—and knowing there's a common thread that binds them together.

When family members make time for each other, work and play together, set goals together, and are willing to listen and help each other, they develop bonds and traditions that strengthen the family in powerful ways. In families today, activities that used to be commonplace, such as being together at mealtimes, working in the garden, going on picnics and hikes, and visiting grandparents, are becoming less and less prevalent. Even the definition of "family" has changed over the decades: today we have everything imaginable, including single-parent, step-, double-income, blended, foster, adoptive, grandparented, and surrogate families and combinations thereof. However, families are forged as much by love and experience as by biology, and so children can feel the unity of a family group regardless of the exact configuration.

Julie and Dave had two children, Noelle, 13, and Erik, 8. Erik's passion was soccer and most other sports, and Noelle was into dance, shopping for clothes, and talking on the phone to her friends. When the family went to Erik's soccer games on Saturday, Noelle never wanted to go; she wanted to stay home and talk to friends or go to the mall. When the family would decide to go to a movie, Noelle no longer wanted to go along—she was afraid some of her friends might see her with her parents. Noelle didn't even want to go on the family vacation and asked if she could stay with a friend instead.

Julie knew that some of what Noelle was feeling was typical for a teenager, but she also felt that it was important for her two children to support each other and for the family to continue to share experiences together. When Julie discussed the problem with Noelle and again tried to encourage her to come to one of Erik's games, Noelle replied that she thought the games were boring and that Erik didn't really care if she came, so why should she waste her time at his game when she could be having fun with her friends.

Determined to work on establishing some sense of cohesiveness within her family, Julie placed a bowl of M&M's on the table after dinner one night and conducted the following activity.

31
Getting to Know You

Group size: 3 or more

Age: 5 and up

Materials: pencil and paper; play money or small candy, such as M&M's

---

Remember your first love and the excitement of that initial period when you were getting to know each other? Each of you spent a great deal of time and energy discovering the other's likes and dislikes, and while differences were acknowledged, those things held in common were celebrated. This game derives its benefits and energy from that discovery process.

For siblings and family members to become better friends, it helps for them to think about their similarities. Children need to find something they have in common on which to build their relationships. Anything you can do to help your children find links between them will help even squabbling siblings feel at least tolerant of each other, and feel some sense of unity within the family.

This game can be done by the whole family, or if you have a large family, you can do it in two or three groups. There should be a minimum of three people in a group.

If you have more than one group, tell everyone to make believe they have a common ancestor, Uncle Jeremiah, who finally died at the age of 120. He was a millionaire, but very strange. He wanted to leave his whole fortune to a group of his descendants, but first he wanted to make sure they were really members of the same family. Uncle Jeremiah would leave his million only to the family that could come up with 30 things they had in common. He figured that if people are part of the same family they must have many similarities.

Give the group or groups a pencil and paper and set a timer. Tell them they have 10 minutes to dig up as many things as possible that they have in common. These might include having brown hair, living in New York, having ten fingers, owning a pair of tennis shoes, going to the same school, or liking chocolate-mint ice cream. The more they come up with, the more fortune they win. They can award two points for every item the entire team shares in common and one point for any item that two or more members share.

Another way to play this is with candy, something like M&M's. Award one M&M for each point. You can have the groups compete against each other to see who collects the most fortune, or if you think that might lead to fighting, simply have each team report its findings at the end of the game, and reward each team with a small award or treat.

Every group will have a different experience with this game, but here are a few things you might talk about after it's over:

- What did we learn from this game?

- Were you surprised that you had so much in common?

- Do you feel closer to each other after playing this game?

- How are our family relationships strengthened by common traits and interests?

✐

Nothing magic happened in Julie and Dave's family after this game, although they seemed to enjoy the challenge of it. But over the next few weeks, Julie tried each of the activities in this chapter, and little by little, she saw Noelle's self-involved attitude soften slightly as they discussed the importance of sticking together as a family.

One Saturday before Erik's game, Noelle came up to him and said she couldn't come to the game that day, but then she handed him a bag of foil-wrapped chocolate soccer balls she had bought at the mall for him to share with his teammates. And the next week when he gave her one of his soccer trading cards with his picture on the front, she put it up on the bulletin board in her room. The seed had been planted . . . the process had started . . . the family was at least talking about "hanging together" more, and Julie felt confident they would continue to make progress.

32
Pulling Together

Group size: 3 or more

Age: 3 and up

Materials: broomstick or mop handle, paper and marker, tape, strong string or cord

*P*rint the words *"family unity"* or *"family togetherness"* on a small piece of paper or poster board. Tape it to the top of a mop handle or broomstick (or even a yardstick). Cut a piece of string two yards long for each member of your family.

Explain that the stick, string, and sign represent family unity and that you're going to learn something important about living together as a family from this activity. Have each member tie his or her string to the stick a little above the midway point. Lay the stick down in the middle of the floor and have your family sit in a circle, spaced evenly apart, around the stick. This will work even if there are only three people in your family. Tell everyone to lay the end of their string down in front of them.

Ask one member to see if he can raise the stick to a standing position by pulling his string alone. He will find that one string doesn't support the stick very well; it will fall over easily. Next, ask another person to join the first to see if two strings can hold the stick up and keep it standing. It may be possible, but the stick will still be unsteady.

Now let everyone pull on their strings to hold the stick in an upright position. You may have to slightly adjust the points at which the strings are tied, but with people pulling from different directions, the pole will stand upright. While it is still standing, ask your family what they can learn from this exercise. Accept all their responses, but try to point out that with everyone "pulling together" your family is able to accomplish more than each person can by herself. With everyone doing his share, working and playing together as a team, your family will be stronger and happier. Ask them if they can think of times when this has actually been the case (maybe cleaning the garage, taking care of the yard, packing the car for a vacation, decorating the Christmas tree).

Now have someone pull the stick toward him with all his strength while the others pull normally. If one person pulls hard enough, the stick will topple over. Ask, "What does this show about family unity?" Again, allow each one to express his own feelings, but point out that one person in the family, if he is selfish or controlling, can destroy the balance and soon spoil the family's feelings of cooperation and togetherness. Use this activity to discuss ways your family members can show support for one another, and how you might strengthen your family's bonds by spending more time together. This would be a good time to get out the family calendar and plan some fun activities or set aside a certain night of the week as "family night."

33
Strength in Numbers

Group size: 2 or more

Age: 3 and up

Materials: rubber band, 20–30 toothpicks or
wooden matches

You can do this with your family or with a class or team.
Begin by asking a child to break a toothpick in half (or
let each member of the family or team break one). The
child will be able to do it quite easily. Now gather at
least eight toothpicks together and wrap the rubber
band around the bundle. Ask the child to break the bundle in half. No matter how hard he tries, the toothpicks
won't break.

Tell the group that the bundle of toothpicks represents your family unit. Ask a child what he can learn
from this activity about unity and sticking together.
Accept any responses, but be sure to underscore the fact
that sometimes one person alone can be "broken"—hurt,
pressured, burdened, distressed, sad. However, with the
strength and support of the whole family together, each
individual becomes more powerful and the group is generally indestructible.

To reinforce this principle, ask a child to take one

toothpick or wooden match and stand it up on a table or counter. This will be virtually impossible. Now take the bundle of toothpicks; if the ends are even, the bundle should be able to stand. Once again, point out that we are like the toothpicks. When we stand together—shoulder to shoulder, side by side—we improve our chances of being able to confront and overcome life's difficult challenges.

This exercise will work well for blended families, with some alterations in the way it's presented. You might show two small bundles of toothpicks joining together to form a new, stronger unit. For families who have experienced divorce, separation, or the death of a parent or child, careful thought should be given to make it appropriate for the situation. In these cases, it would be wise to discuss how any size family (even a family that has lost one of its members) should be considered a family unit and can still feel a great sense of companionship and strength.

Another way of presenting this idea is to show the children all the separate ingredients that go into a cake. Ask if the flour alone tastes like a cake, or the eggs alone, or the shortening alone. Then ask what you have to do to make it taste like a cake. While you mix together the ingredients, talk about the fact that a family is not really a family if the members are always on their own. It's the mixing together, the interaction, the emotional closeness that blends individuals together and makes them a real family.

34
The Right Moves

Group size: 2 or more

Age: 6 and up

Materials: blindfold; chair; clear plastic drinking glass; pitcher of water, partly full

*B*lindfold one person and give her a pitcher half full of water to hold. Have the other person sit in a chair and give him an empty glass. Tell him to tilt back his head and place the glass on his forehead, open side up.

The blindfolded child with the pitcher should stand a few feet from the chair. Tell the person in the chair that he must instruct the person with the pitcher to pour water into the glass on his head. He must give specific directions to the blindfolded person as to which direction to walk, how high to raise the pitcher, how much to tilt the pitcher, and exactly when to pour, with the least amount of spillage on his head.

The two people may talk freely back and forth, about which way the child should move, how high she should raise her arm, etc. After they have successfully performed this stunt, have them switch places, to experience being in the other person's position.

This activity teaches some important principles about teamwork, cooperation, working together toward a common goal, and communication. As a matter of fact, a whole discussion can come from this experience just about communication. It also can help a child begin to feel empathy for other people, as he experiences what it's like to put himself in someone else's shoes.

35

Spinning a Yarn

Group size: 4 or more

Age: 5 and up

Materials: ball of yarn

---

*T*his game works best if you have 4 or more people—prefer-ably 5 to 10. Have everyone stand in a circle and spread out so there is a space of about three or four feet between each person and the next. Tell your family that you will be tossing the ball of yarn, and whoever catches it has to tell one of the following:

- Something she likes about the person who threw her the ball

- Something she is thankful for

- Something nice the person who threw her the ball has done for her

Take the ball of yarn and toss it to someone in the circle, while holding onto the end so the yarn will unwind. That person will make a statement in one of the above categories and then, while holding onto the yarn, will toss the ball to someone else in the circle. That person will also make one of the three types of statements above about the person who tossed the yarn. Keep this going until everyone in the group has had a chance to share at least one time (several times is best, especially for a small group).

After you have made a spiderweb pattern with the yarn and everyone has had a chance to share, stop the ball. Mention that the effect of sharing positive thoughts and compliments with each other has created a beautiful "web" among the family members. In order for that lovely pattern to evolve, everyone had to participate.

Now ask, "What is this yarn doing for us physically?" Answers should focus on the idea of "holding us together" or unifying the family. Next, ask one or two members of the group to drop the yarn. Immediately the center web will become loose. Then ask, "What happens to the group when someone drops his yarn?" (It becomes less close, less closely knit, and it makes something beautiful fall apart and become weak.)

Discuss how this is like a family. Some points may be that we will function better as a family if we bear each other's burdens, lift and support each other, share our joys and sorrows, and are thankful for each other and all that we have. Emphasize that in sharing feelings with each other, a beautiful network of relationships and ties is formed, just like what is physically illustrated by the yarn, but that it takes everyone doing his or her part to hold it together.

PART NINE
Gratitude

For the children:

True wealth is what you are, not what you have.

For the parents:

A man travels the world over in search of what he needs and returns home to find it.

—*George Moore*

Dear God,

I didn't think orange went with purple until I saw the sunset you made on Tuesday. That was cool.

—Eugene

A family interviewed recently on the *Today* show had just driven across two thirds of the United States to reach New York City. They had seen the Grand Canyon, Mt. Rushmore, and many other landmarks on their way. When the 12-year-old daughter was asked what was the best thing she had seen on the trip, she immediately responded, "The Great Mall" (a new supersize mall in the Midwest).

We live in a glorious universe, surrounded by miracles of nature, but in our fast-paced, supersophisticated world, we too often take the beauty of the earth, and the people on it, for granted. The colors and textures of our lives blur before us like a movie run in fast motion as we dash from one scene to the next. Unless we take the time to help our children embrace the world in which they live, they'll acquiesce to the "mall mentality" and grow up being more preoccupied with wanting what they don't have than appreciating what they have.

Consider for a moment the reflections of another 12-year-old girl, Emily in Thornton Wilder's play *Our Town*, when she is allowed to look back from heaven at one day of her life—her twelfth birthday:

I can't look at everything hard enough. Wait! One more look. Good-bye, good-bye, world. Good-bye, Grover's Corners . . . Mama and Papa. Good-bye to clocks ticking

*and Mama's sunflowers. And food . . . and new-ironed
dresses and hot baths . . . and sleeping and waking up.
Oh, earth, you're too wonderful for anybody to realize
you. Do any human beings ever realize life while they
live it, every, every minute?*

A grateful heart is one of the greatest gifts you can
give yourself and your children. Cicero called gratitude
"the mother of all virtues," because it gives our days a
keener edge and our lives a more gracious touch. We
can give this gift to our children in very simple ways—
standing with them at the beach, letting the gentle
waves pull at your feet; climbing up a mountainside
with the wind blowing in your face; watching the forces
of the whole universe played out in one tiny anthill;
feeling the soft fur on a kitten's chest; singing songs at
the top of your lungs; letting the juice of a watermelon
run down your chin; laughing together until your stom-
achs hurt—and then letting your children hear you
express gratitude for all those common things, and for
them.

Perhaps the most significant way to teach gratitude to
your children is to allow them to experience receiving
it: praise them, appreciate them, compliment them. It's
too easy to focus on the negative with kids, and not even
see the good things they do, let alone comment on them.
How often do you walk into the family room and say,
"Thanks for doing the dishes without my asking,"
instead of the standard, "All right, you guys, who left this
mess out?" If you get into the habit of expressing appreciation for your children, they will be more inclined to
express appreciation to their siblings, friends, teachers,
and eventually their own spouses and children.

An ancient Jewish legend says that the world will only be complete when everyone can identify one hundred blessings in their lives each day. It's an idea we would be wise to incorporate into our parenting style—to look for one hundred opportunities each day to tell our children positive things about their behavior and to communicate how important and valuable they are as human beings, and how much they are loved. Many of us would find it a challenge to comply with one tenth of what the legend teaches, but making the effort even to some degree can literally transform your relationship with your children and the entire atmosphere in your home.

We can teach our children that they can make a difference in the life of another human being by a simple word of gratitude. There is a poignant story of a woman who had been a schoolteacher her whole life and who, after retirement, received a letter of appreciation from one of her students. This was her reply to him:

My dear Jake:

I cannot tell you how much your note meant. I am in my eighties, living alone in a small room, cooking my own meals, lonely, and like the last leaf that falls— lingering behind. You will be interested to know that I taught school for fifty years and yours was the first note of appreciation I ever received. It came on a blue, cold morning, and it cheered me as nothing else has for many years.

In today's affluent society, it's easy for our children to become jaded, taking all the comforts of their lives and the people who enrich them for granted. A mother of two young children, Laura Lewis, recently told me about her daughter Olivia, age six, who asked for soda pop instead of milk to go with her dinner one night. She had just returned from staying with her grandparents, who regularly served soft drinks with their meals. Olivia kept complaining when her mother refused to give it to her, until her mother finally said in exasperation, "Olivia, if you want soft drinks with dinner, you'll have to go live with Grandma and Grandpa."

Olivia considered the proposition seriously for a minute and then bluntly responded, "No, Mommy, Grandma's TV screen isn't big enough!" Laura and her husband were a bit unsettled by the reply, and decided right then and there to find some ways to help their children become more appreciative of the abundance in their lives. Laura began by conducting the activity called Around the World, modified and greatly simplified, to meet her small family's needs.

36
Around the World

Group size: 6 or more

Age: 3 and up

Materials: paper plates; rice, beans, tortillas; a prepared dinner; china, silverware; pieces of paper (one for each game participant); a bowl

---

When a child was asked what Thanksgiving was like at his house, he answered, "All the dads watch football all day, the moms wash the dishes, we say grace and chew with our mouths closed." If you want to provide a different experience some Thanksgiving, one that your family will never forget, try this activity. It will take a little forethought and preparation, but your children will talk about it for years to come. Although it can be done on Thanksgiving Day, it is probably easier to do on another day during the Thanksgiving season or on any other day of the year.

This experience is best done with a fairly large group of people—10 or more, if possible—and it will work with any group larger than that. It's possible to do it with a small family of four, as well, but it works better when a group of friends or extended family are gathered together. First, prepare enough rice for about half the group. Prepare a small serving of tortillas and beans for about one third of the group, in addition to having a regular meal prepared for the entire group.

On each piece of paper write down the name of a different country of the world and the category to which it belongs (First World, Second World, Third World—terms indicating economic levels, used for the purpose of this activity). There should be the same number of papers as people present. The countries written on the papers should be in the following categories, in these proportions:

Third World, one half of the papers: such countries as India, China, Ethiopia, Iran, Pakistan, Nigeria

Second World, one third of the papers: such countries as Mexico, Peru, Guatemala, Russia, Samoa, Israel

First World, one sixth of the papers: such countries as the United States, Canada, Australia, Japan, France, Great Britain

If 24 people are in the group, the Third World would have 12 papers (one half), the Second World would have 8 papers (one third), and the First World would have 4 papers (one sixth). If there are 6 people in your group, there would be 3 papers in the Third World, 2 papers in the Second World, and 1 paper in the First World.

Fold the papers and put them into the bowl. Have each person pick a piece of paper and announce what country he or she is "from." After everyone has a country, tell them that they will now be served what the majority of people from their "homeland" will be eating for dinner that night. On paper plates, serve a scoop of rice to the people in the Third World. Tell them to go outside and sit on the ground and eat their dinner. Serve a tortilla with a small amount of beans to Second World people and ask them to sit outside at a picnic table or at your kitchen table. The person or few people in the First World will be served a regular meal on dinnerware at a nice table, perhaps in the dining area.

When we did this activity, we scheduled it one or two hours before our regular dinner, so appetites wouldn't be spoiled. We also didn't serve an entire meal to the First World people, but rather some hors d'oeuvres and soup. We naturally prepared enough of the "real thing" for the whole group, but pretended at the time that their "country" portions would be their entire dinner.

This is a very effective and sobering way to teach your family gratitude for all they have as a result of their living in America; even the poorest among us are far better off than most people in the rest of the world. Depending on the ages of the children, this might be a good time to discuss what it would be like to live in another country: the living conditions, the food, the government, the education available, the opportunities, the working conditions, the freedom of religion, the right to vote or the lack of it, etc.

The night Laura tried this with her family, she invited her parents over for dinner. There were six people, so three got countries in the Third World, two got Second

World countries, and one person got a First World country. Laura made sure her daughter Olivia got a country from the Third World. When Olivia received her scoop of rice, she asked if there was any meat, salad, potatoes, or drink to go with it, and wondered why her dad (the one who got the First World) got pork chops and mashed potatoes for dinner. Her mother and grandfather (the two other people in the Third World) took her outside to sit on the grass and eat their rice.

While they ate, they talked to Olivia about how some children live in other countries and showed her pictures Laura had borrowed from the library of the children in parts of Africa, the location of Olivia's country. She was disgruntled at first, not even touching her rice, but as she looked at the pictures, she started asking questions about whether these children went to school, whether they had ever watched TV or gone to a movie, whether they shopped at stores for clothes or toys, what books they might have read, and whether they got to eat anything different from the bowl of rice for breakfast or lunch.

The evening seemed to have a genuine effect on Olivia and although she felt hungry and thirsty an hour later, she didn't complain too much. Laura gave her a sandwich and milk before she went to bed, and they talked about the experience as Laura tucked her in that night.

Olivia is still a normal child who continues to expect too much at times, but she often brings up the experience of that evening and the feelings she had for the less fortunate children in other parts of the world. And she is happy *to be able* to drink milk with her dinner now.

37
A Touch of Gratitude

Group size: 2 or more

Age: 4 and up

Materials: 1 men's tube sock; cylindrical container 6–12 inches high and 4–6 inches in diameter (large soup can, plastic tube, oatmeal box, hot chocolate can); small objects around the house

*T*his is a fun game to remind children of all the things in life for which they should be grateful. Before you start, gather 8 to 12 small objects from around the house that represent "blessings" in life. Some ideas are:

Object	Blessings It Represents
Small blossom	Flowers and beautiful plants
Toy animal	Variety of animals for many different purposes (food and pets)
Carrot	Food to eat
Doll clothes	Clothes to wear
Small ball or toy	Fun and recreation in life

Pencil	Gift of being able to write
Paper	Ability to record and pass down information/history
Toy car	Cars and transportation
Tiny book	Books, knowledge, education
Small soap	Soap and sanitation (to maintain health)
Small Christmas light	Electricity
Bandage or aspirin	Medicine and doctors
Dollar bill or coin	Money to buy things
Small doll	People around us—family, friends
Leaf	Trees
Sun (small cutout)	Sunshine
Raindrop (small cutout)	Rain

The list is endless, limited only by your imagination and what you have available. Place all the items in the can. Stretch the tube sock over the can so that the toe of the sock is snug around the bottom of the can. There should be a long section of the sock hanging from the top of the can or jar, through which a child can put his hand, creating a "mystery can" because the objects will not be visible. Place all the items in the can before beginning the activity.

The child puts his hand into the opening of the sock, down into the can, and feels for one object, and must tell you what he thinks the object is before he pulls it out through the opening of the sock. After he takes it out, he must tell you what gift or blessing he thinks it represents. If there is more than one child, have them take turns reaching for objects. You can keep score if you desire, giving a point each time the child correctly identifies the object, and another point if he can tell what it represents.

For older children, after they have identified the blessing represented by the object, ask them to describe what life would be like without that blessing, or discuss how some people today live without it, or talk about people in history who have survived without it and how their lives were different.

Children really love this game, not only for the chance it gives them to think about all the good things in their lives but also because it's fun to test their sense of touch for identifying things.

38

The Happiness Test

Group size: 2 or more

Age: 7 and up

Materials: pencils, a copy of this test or plain paper

---

*I*f your children ever complain about not having a new car, a swimming pool, the latest-style clothes, or about not being able to go on an elaborate vacation every year, give them the following test. You can make copies of this or simply read the questions aloud and have them mark their answers on a blank sheet of paper.

1. Over 700 million people in the world are now judged by the United Nations to be hungry or starving. Do you have plenty of different kinds of food to eat?
   Yes_____ No_____
   When was the last time you really felt hungry for longer than eight hours, without being able to eat something?

   _____

2. Over 500 million people in the world (more than all the people in the United States) do not have a permanent

weatherproof shelter to live in. Do you have a permanent home to live in?

Yes_____ No_____

How many rooms are in your house or apartment?

_____

3. Only 1 person out of every 7,000 in the world has a TV to watch. Do you have a TV to entertain you?

Yes_____ No_____

How many TVs do you have in your home? _____

4. Over 800 million people in the world have only one set of clothes to wear. Many more than that have no shoes, no coat, no underwear. Do you have enough different kinds of clothes to wear?

Yes_____ No_____

How many pair of shoes do you own? _____

5. Over 700 million people in the world die every year because they have no doctor or medicine. When you get sick, is there a doctor and medicine to help you get well?

Yes_____ No_____

6. Only 1 out of every 8,000 people in the world has a refrigerator and stove in the home. Is there a refrigerator and stove in your home?

Yes_____ No_____

Is there a microwave?_____a dryer?_____ a toaster?_____ a garbage disposal? _____

7. Over 450 million people in the world do not own a radio or a cassette, record, or CD player. Do you have a radio or

stereo system in your home?

Yes_____ No_____

How many?_____

8. Only 1 out of every 750 children in the world has the chance to learn to read and write and do arithmetic. Do you have a chance to learn to read, write, and do arithmetic?

Yes_____ No_____

How many books do you have in your house? _____

How many books have you read this year?_____

9. Only 1 out of 760 million people in this world has hot and cold running water and a private indoor bathroom in the home. Do you have these things?

Yes_____ No_____

How many bathrooms do you have in your house?_____

How many hot baths or showers do you get to take per week?_____

10. Over 960 million people in the world have no restaurants of any kind available to them. Is there a McDonald's or other kind of restaurant in your community?

Yes_____ No _____

How many restaurants or fast-food chains can you name that you have been to in the past year? _____

How many times per month do you eat out at restaurants or fast-food places?_____

Teach your children that we should be grateful for all we have. And because we have been given so much, we should repay our families, our friends, our neighbors, and the world in whatever small ways we can. Here are a few very basic ways we can show our gratitude to those close to us. See how well you score in your consideration of others:

If you OPEN it, do you CLOSE it?

Yes_____ No_____ Sometimes_____

If you turn it ON, do you turn it OFF?

Yes_____ No_____ Sometimes_____

If you UNLOCK it, do you LOCK it again?

Yes_____ No_____ Sometimes_____

If you BREAK it, do you REPAIR it?

Yes_____ No_____ Sometimes_____

If you cannot FIX it, do you REPORT it?

Yes_____ No_____ Sometimes_____

If it BELONGS to someone else, do you get PERMISSION first?

Yes_____ No_____ Sometimes_____

If you BORROW it, do you RETURN it?

Yes_____ No_____ Sometimes_____

If you make a MESS, do you CLEAN it up?

Yes_____ No_____ Sometimes_____

If you MOVE it, do you PUT IT BACK?

Yes_____ No_____ Sometimes_____

Score

2 points for each "yes"
1 point for each "sometimes"
Subtract 1 point for each "no"

14–18 points: You are very considerate of others and are probably a good example to those around you.

9–13 points: You are moderately considerate of others, but need to take more responsibility for your actions.

0–8 points: You need to take a serious look at how you can be more respectful of others and more grateful for your belongings.

39
Uncovering Blessings

Group size: 2 or more

Age: 4 and up

Materials: saucer, plastic spoon, salt*, black pepper, piece of woolen cloth

*F*ill a saucer with about half a cup of salt. Have a child sprinkle some pepper over it, enough so that you can see some flecks. After he has stirred it around a little, tell him to hold the plastic spoon over the salt and pepper— not touching it but close to it. Nothing should happen. Now have the child rub the spoon with the woolen cloth. Tell him to hold the spoon over the salt and pepper again; this time the pepper should be attracted to and stick to the spoon. If all the pepper isn't drawn out of the salt, you may have to wipe the existing pepper off the spoon and rub it with the cloth again.

Explain that the pepper represents the blessings in our lives. Sometimes our blessings are difficult to see and seem outnumbered by our problems or what we lack (the salt). Many times when people examine their lives (the spoon "looking over" the salt and pepper) they

---

*This activity is also very effective with a magnet and sand that contains iron shavings.

forget the abundance of good things they possess and instead focus on what they don't have. This causes them to feel empty (the bare spoon). If they stop to think about the good people, relationships, the beauty of nature, and the conveniences in their lives, their hearts will "warm up" (the wool cloth rubbing the spoon), and their hearts will be changed into grateful hearts. They will then be able to recognize the many blessings for which they should be thankful (the pepper now clinging to the spoon).

PART TEN

Courage and Adversity

For the children:

Life sometimes gives you the test before you've had
a chance to study the lesson.

For the parents:

Courage is the ability to go from one failure to
another without losing your enthusiasm.

Once upon a time a long, long time ago, I used to cook breakfast for my family. I remember one morning when my son Seth came down to the table, looked at the scrambled eggs, wheat toast, and orange juice, and said, "But, Mom, I ordered three chocolate donuts and a side of hash-browns!"

Seth had always been my "laughing place," but this particular wisecrack provided some real food for thought. If you think of life as if it were a series of meals, most of us will go through it not getting exactly what we ordered. While everything we could possibly dream of is on the menu—good health, fun, love, success, wealth, beauty—life, like my family's breakfast table, is not a "made-to-order" situation, and that's probably a good thing. What a soft lot we would all be if we lived on a constant diet of donuts and hash-browns, or the other indulgences of our choosing.

Instead, life serves up a variety of experiences for children as well as adults, some of which may not be sweet to the taste but may provide the nourishment needed for proper growth and development. Sometimes we are served entrees of illness, loneliness, failure, or abuse, along with side dishes of peer pressure, accident, injury, divorce or death. At those times we find ourselves wanting to shout, "But this isn't what I ordered! I ordered fun and happiness and good health! The waiter must've made a mistake! Take it back!" But he almost never does.

We soon learn that these bittersweet experiences in life are what help us develop courage and backbone. If we are open to learning from them, they will give us the "muscle" we need to deal with hard times and misfortune. We cannot *give* courage to our children and we can't force it on them. It is something they have to find for themselves within themselves. We can, however, show them by example what it is and how it feels, and we can praise them when we notice their own attempts at being courageous.

Many parents have the tendency to want to protect their children from challenging situations. They don't want to see their kids suffer, and they attempt to manipulate the world so that their children won't be exposed to too much pain. A child is much like a new chick coming out of its shell. He pokes his beak out first, and with his egg tooth he pecks a crack around the circumference of the shell. Then, over a period of hours or days, the tiny chick develops the muscle to hook its feet into the crack and finally push the shell fragments apart.

A concerned human being watching this process for the first time might feel sorry for the struggling chick. In an effort to assist it, the person might gently peel away parts of the shell to ease the chick's labor, thereby shortening the hatching process. Anyone who has ever tried this, however, realizes his mistake when, just a few hours later, the chick usually dies. What the person didn't understand is that the muscle and stamina developed by the chick during its natural hatching process is the same vigor needed to survive on its own. Deprived of that experience, the chick can't survive out of the shell. In a similar way, parents must stand back and allow certain struggles to occur in their children's lives, in order for the children to develop strong, resilient personalities.

Every family's needs will be different, but the next time one of your children needs a shot of courage or a clearer picture of her inner strength, try one of the following activities.

40

Rock Solid

Group size: 2 or more

Age: 5 and up

Materials: a heavy rock, an inflated balloon, small board with a nail driven through it, marker

*B*efore you begin, write the words "life's problems" or, for an older group, "adversity" on the small board. Explain that the balloon and the rock represent two types of people or two different ways the same person might act. The rock has a few rough edges, it's not perfectly shaped, its color is dull, and it's heavy. The balloon, on the other hand, is light, round, colorful, and smooth.

Ask the children what the personalities of these two "people" might be like. How would they act with a group of friends? Which one would tend to be bossy? Which would be more likely to care about the needs of others? Let them respond however they see fit and discuss accordingly. It doesn't really matter if they visualize the different personalities correctly at this point—the questions are just to get them thinking about the two objects as people.

Now introduce the board with the nail. Ask the children what some problems in life might be (sickness, financial problems, loneliness, problems with friends, school difficulties, divorce, moving to a new city, death of a pet). With younger children you might want to choose one specific experience, like going to a new school, and talk about how that challenge would make the child feel.

Scratch the rock with the point of the nail. Then hit the rock in different spots hard with the nail, and ask what is happening to this "person" as he is confronted with and attacked by problems in his life. (He can feel the pain of the nail, and it might leave some scratches here and there, but he is not destroyed by life's problems.)

Take the board with the nail and touch the balloon gently with it. Tap a little here and there, and then press harder until the balloon bursts.

Discuss why the balloon was destroyed so much more quickly than the rock. Ask:

- Which "person" has a more solid foundation?

- How long did it take for the rock to be formed in the first place?

- What's inside the balloon? Does its colorful, perfectly shaped exterior help out when the "balloon" person is under pressure?

- What made these objects weak or strong when faced with adversity? (What are they really made of? What is inside?)

- What is meant by the term "hot air"?

Now ask each child how she can become the type of person who won't "pop under pressure" immediately, and who will have the courage and fortitude to remain strong and solid even when faced with stress and challenges in life. You might give examples of specific challenges and ask the child what she could do to remain "solid" when confronted by those trials.

41

What Would You Do If?

Group size: 2 or more

Age: 3 and up

Materials: None

*T*his very simple game has more potential to teach important lessons to your children than perhaps any other game in the book. It is one that requires no planning and no equipment and works great in the car, on an airplane, at the mall or grocery store when you're shopping, or almost anywhere you find yourself with a restless or bored child. I played it with each of my children over and over again through the years and they never got tired of it. They were so relentless in their requests for this game at certain ages that it was a challenge for me to keep coming up with new material.

This is an activity that helps children of all ages develop problem-solving and decision-making skills, which in turn help them develop self-confidence. And children cannot develop mental toughness and courage without self-confidence. This little game also helps them rehearse their reactions to real-life situations.

All that is involved is asking your child a series of questions you make up as you go along, beginning each series of questions with "What would you do if . . . ?" After each of the child's answers, encourage discussion of the scenario and follow up with questions like, "What else could you do?" or "What if that didn't work?" If you're concerned about a child's inappropriate response, tell her how you would solve the problem and ask for her opinion on it.

There is no limit to the kinds of questions you can ask. Here's a list of questions to get you started. Sometimes my questions have been based on the season (such as scary Halloween questions or gift-related problems at Christmastime), sometimes they have been pure fun and fantasy, and sometimes the questions have been perplexing and thought-provoking. Regardless of the type of question, I believe my children have consistently learned as much from thinking about them as I have learned from their answers.

What Would You Do If . . .

1. You were at the mall and you turned around and couldn't find your mother anywhere?

2. Your friend at school showed you a watch he had taken out of someone else's desk?

3. Someone came to your school and told you that your mother had asked him to pick you up because her car had broken down?

4. You were out trick-or-treating on Halloween and an older kid in costume told you to come and see something behind some trees?

5. You had very little money at Christmastime and your best friend gave you a very expensive gift?

6. You were sleeping overnight at a friend's house and he put on an R-rated movie, the viewing of which was against your family's rules?

7. You were walking down the block and found a wallet with a fifty-dollar bill in it and no identification?

8. While playing baseball in a vacant lot, you hit a hard ball and it accidentally dented the hood of a car parked nearby?

9. You were in charge of a spaceship crew of five people that would be gone for five months; you left Earth two days ago, and suddenly you realize there is only enough food on board for three people for the five months?

10. You were riding your bike home from school with a friend and he fell off his bike and was bleeding?

11. You were asleep and a fire alarm woke you up?

12. A friend invited you over to play games and then another friend called and asked you to come over swimming the same afternoon?

13. A girl from Germany came to your school. She didn't understand how to play the games at recess and was sitting alone on the bench?

14. At school, an older kid trips you on the playground; you fall and break your tooth on the cement. The next day, the boy comes up and apologizes?

15. You are watching your favorite TV show and your mom asks you to go out to the car and bring the groceries in?

Again, this list is just to prompt your thinking. For very young children, the questions could be about sharing toys, obeying their parents, etc. The possibilities are endless.

42

On a Roll

Group size: 2 or more

Age: 4 and up

Materials: 1 sheet of typing paper, 1 small book

Show the child the piece of paper and ask him if there is any way the paper can hold up the book, if he uses only one hand to hold the paper. The child may try, or may automatically realize there is no way.

Now take the paper and roll it tightly into a tube, the diameter of which should be about 1 to 1 ½ inches. Hold the tube in one hand and carefully place the book on top of the open end of the tube. It should support the book.

Relate this to the ability we each have of turning our weaknesses into strengths. The paper at first is flimsy, weak, lacking backbone and character—easy to crush and overwhelm. This might be compared to some people who are faced with a problem or obstacle: they may lack the courage to confront the problem or stand up to the opposition.

In a sense, they have a weakness—it might be fear, insecurity, or a prior failure that worries them. A child who strikes out every time at bat has a fear that he will never be able to hit the ball; that fear becomes a paralyzing weakness.

There are ways we can turn our weaknesses into strengths. Through practice, determination, patience, and perseverance, we can improve and sharpen our skills. Just as the paper can be rolled into a sturdy tube, we can work to add muscle to our frailties if we have the courage to persist. We will thereby develop the fortitude and backbone to hold up under pressure.

Ask the child to tell what someone could do to turn the following weaknesses into strengths:

- Tommy has to give a speech in class and is afraid to speak in front of his classmates.

- Jenny loves ice cream and cookies but she has gained 10 pounds in the last year and is somewhat overweight for her age.

- Karen was born blind and, at age seven, goes to a special school. Lately her parents have noticed her sitting at the piano making up her own simple melodies.

- Steven is in junior high and his grades are below average. He's not very popular and he doesn't feel good about himself. The only thing he seems interested in is photography.

- Jeffrey is extra short for his age, 10. He loves basketball but has always been timid about signing up for a team, thinking that his skills wouldn't measure up.

In most of these cases, there are things the parents could do to encourage turning the child's weaknesses into strengths. When we as parents become aware of certain shortcomings or fears in our children, we need to help them discover ways to face those fears and then provide the encouragement and support to help them make changes.

And when they fail, which they will occasionally, we should remind the child that courage comes in the attempts, not necessarily in the accomplishment. Many courageous moments in life come on the heels of a failure from which the child receives encouragement to try again. If we praise children for trying, we will be helping them to build a deep and enduring courage.

43

A Crushing Blow

Group size: 2 or more

Age: 3 and up

Materials: soda crackers, rolling pin, paper, marker, cutting board

---

*F*ear is a very powerful emotion that can defeat a child's self-confidence. This activity will empower your child to overcome his fears and become more aware of the qualities that should give him courage.

First, talk with your child about his fears. You might have to prompt his thinking by asking questions like, "Is there anything in your room that scares you? . . . What do you like least about going to school? . . . Why don't you like playing at Johnny's house? . . . What is it about 'show and tell' that worries you?"

With a marking pen, draw on a cracker a simple symbol or the first letter of the word that describes each of the fears you identify. Now talk about the weapons your child has that can conquer fear, and write them on a piece of paper.

Think of his innate abilities—things like being a fast runner, being good at solving puzzles, his alert mind, his ability to handle emergencies well, his natural ability to care for animals, his power to concentrate, his good hand-eye coordination, etc. You can find noble characteristics and turn them into effective "battle weapons" if you use your imagination. The possibilities are limitless, for within every child are many unique abilities; we just need to take the time to explore them.

After you have written down these qualities, talk about how each is stronger than the fear itself. When enlisted into service and strategically put into action, these natural abilities can conquer fear and anxiety. Wrap the piece of paper around the rolling pin and secure it with tape.

First ask your child if he can blow away the fear crackers. He will blow on them and they may move slightly, but they will still remain mostly intact.

Now have the child grasp the handles of the rolling pin and crush the crackers on the cutting board with all his strength. Kids love to do this anyway, but will really get behind it with this new meaning attached. Now, to show that fear is more easily destroyed after it has been broken down, ask him to blow away the crushed crumbs. He will easily be able to do it and will watch his fears get blown away.

PART ELEVEN

Respect and Manners

For the children:

Good manners sometimes means simply putting up with other people's bad manners.

For the parents:

Treat a man as he is, and he will remain as he is. Treat him as he could be, and he will become what can and should be.

—*Goethe*

I was enlightened once by a conversation between my sons, Ian and Alex, ages 10 and 7 at the time, over a piece of cake. There were two pieces left—one big and one not so big. As Alex snatched the bigger one, Ian said, "Alex, where are your manners? If *I* choose first, I always take the *smaller* piece of cake." To which Alex quipped, "I knew that. That's why I saved it for you!"

It's one of the most fundamental lessons in life to teach our kids—to honor and respect the feelings of every other person in the world. It's also a quality that doesn't exactly come naturally to children. A young child considers the needs of only one person—himself. So for a while, parents need to serve as moral stand-ins, helping their children distinguish the right and wrong way to treat others.

As kids get a little older, they begin to acknowledge the needs of those around them and display a certain tolerance for those needs, but the ability to show *real* caring and respect for others is a learned quality that takes years to develop. They *say* children finally begin to develop a genuine sensitivity toward family members and friends when they hit their teen years. . . . No comment.

What I *will* comment on, however, is the one thing that remains unchanged and constant in *all* families—children develop personal character traits by modeling themselves on the adults in their lives. They will learn their first lessons in how they should treat people by watching how their parents treat people. When children notice parents who are thoughtful and generous, dependable and kind, who love deeply and demonstrably, they not only learn how to act in their own personal relationships, but how to respect, care about, and love *all* people.

Our neighbor Nick is handicapped and in a wheelchair. His legs are withered and his speech is haltingly awkward. Nick has lived down the block for 10 years now, since he was six, and on any typical Saturday afternoon, you will see him go from house to house, knocking on each door, hoping to find someone who will spend a few minutes talking with him about his favorite subject, sports.

Not everyone has time for Nick. But I've watched my husband on numerous occasions stand at the front door for more than a half hour joking and laughing with him, discussing everything from high school football to the Special Olympics. And over the years, I have watched each of my children follow their father's lead. It's not always convenient, but I don't notice any of my kids closing the door on Nick. And someday they'll recognize what they've learned by observing their father—that the true test of character is not in how we treat our boss, our favorite teacher, or our best friend. The true measure of character is in how we treat the person who has nothing obvious to give us in return. More times than not, those people actually give us something back, as Nick has done by demonstrating great courage and determination in overcoming the obstacles in his life.

The secret to raising kids who will end up being respectful, courteous, and polite to others is to show respect to those children. Linda and Richard Eyre, the authors of *Teaching Your Children Values*, observe: "The main thing to remember is that respect isn't *given* consistently unless it is *received*. . . . The respect [children] *receive* in the home will be the basis for their own self-respect; and the respect they learn to *show* in the home will be the foundation on which to build respect for others outside the home." In the midst of the blaming, criticizing, lecturing routine in which we too often find ourselves with our children, we need to stop and ask ourselves, "If I treated my friends the way I treat my children, would I have any friends left?"

Even the best of friends will have moments of both sublime exhilaration and disillusionment. Learning how to be a good friend can be difficult, but we can assist our children in this endeavor by teaching them to be empathic and sensitive toward their friends.

Samantha and Annie were in the fifth grade and had been best friends for three years. They did everything together and could almost read each other's minds. But one day Annie came to school and was extra quiet. She sat on a bench during recess and didn't talk much to Samantha. When Samantha approached her, Annie turned away with a painful look on her face.

The next day, things were the same and Samantha was feeling hurt, thinking Annie didn't want to be friends anymore. She planned to call Annie after school to tell her how upset she was. When Samantha got home, she confided in her mom, who listened and then suggested they play The Golden Rule before she called Annie.

44
The Golden Rule

Group size: 3 or more

Age: 4 and up

Materials: 2 pictures of the same type of object (cut out of magazines), poster board, glue or tape

---

*B*efore you begin, cut out two pictures from magazines of the same type of object (a baby, a house, a car, a fish, a boat, a tree, etc.) shown in two different contexts. For example, one picture of a tree might be of a Christmas tree covered with lights and one might be a *National Geographic*–style close-up of one branch of a tree with bugs crawling on the leaves.

Glue or tape the two pictures to the two sides of a piece of poster board or heavy paper. Ask two family members to stand facing each other about six feet apart. Bring out the poster and hold it between them so that each person is looking at a different side.

Tell them you have a picture of the same item taped to both sides of the poster. Ask the two people to take turns describing one feature of the object he sees without telling what the object is (it has bricks, it has brown eyes, it's a circular shape, etc.). After both have responded, and they begin to realize they're talking about different things, ask why there might be a discrepancy between the two views. Ask one of them how he might resolve this disagreement. If they can't come up with a solution, give the following possibilities: 1) tell the other person he is wrong; 2) argue with him and insist that your description is correct; 3) come around to the other side and trying to see the picture from the other person's point of view.

Hopefully, the family will decide the third choice is wisest. Have one person walk around and look at the other side of the poster. Then ask your family members some of the following questions:

- Why is it important to see things from the other person's point of view?

- Why do people often argue about something instead of attempting to see the other side?

- Who benefits from seeing the other person's point of view?

- What is the Golden Rule and what does it teach us to do?

- Does obeying the Golden Rule help us avoid arguments? How?

- Can you think of a time you knew you were right about something and someone disagreed with you? How did you resolve it? Were you willing to listen to the other person's opinion and try to see it from his standpoint?

- What does it mean to "walk in someone else's shoes"?

After this activity, Samantha tried to think about things from Annie's perspective in an effort to understand what could have caused her negative attitude over the past two days. She started to wonder if something bad might have happened to her, and instead of calling her to tell her how hurt she was, she decided to make some brownies and take them to Annie's house.

When she arrived, Annie's mother said Annie was asleep. She then explained that her dog had died two days before, and Annie was having a very hard time dealing with the loss. She said every time Annie thought about it, she started crying, and so she was trying not to talk to anyone about it, in an effort to control her emotions. Now Samantha understood, and was glad her mother had helped her think things through before she had made a potentially damaging phone call.

45
Bag of Feathers

Group size: 2 or more

Ages: 4 and up

Materials: paper bag; feathers (rice or birdseed also work); a windy day, if possible; chopsticks (optional); a bedsheet (optional)

Go outside with your child or family and sit in an open area. Begin by talking briefly about having good manners and respecting other people. Put the feathers into the paper sack and hand it to a child. Allow her to open the bag and freely toss the contents all around the area. As she does so, personally "instruct" the feathers not to go any farther; tell them to stay put where they first land.

Discuss how the feathers are like gossip or talking behind someone's back. The feathers are easily scattered about and will blow from place to place, even if they are instructed to stay put; it's very easy to say things about other people and to spread rumors. It's even kind of fun sometimes to be the first to tell something "juicy" about someone else. But we find that even when we ask someone not to tell anyone else, the gossip spreads and spreads, just as the feathers blow from place to place even when "told" not to.

Now tell the child to go collect the feathers. She may look at you like you're crazy, but be insistent. After she's at least made an attempt to collect the feathers, ask her whether it was easy to locate all the feathers. Compare this to the effects of gossip: repeating bad things or spreading rumors about other people is easy to do but very difficult to gather up or take back once the rumors have been disseminated.

Most people won't have a bag of feathers handy, but this works with rice or birdseed and chopsticks. Scatter the rice all around the area and then ask the family members to use chopsticks or their fingers to retrieve each grain of rice. Talk about the difficulty of this task and compare it to the difficulty of retrieving unkind words that have been freely tossed about.

An amusing follow-up game to this activity is the "feather blowing game." This is fun if you have four or more people in your group. Ask everyone to stand in a big circle and spread out a bedsheet in the middle of the group (twin size for a small group, queen or king size for 10 or more people).

Tell everyone to pick up an edge of the sheet and hold it with both hands under their chin, pulling the sheet tight in all directions. One person then tosses a feather out on top of the sheet and everyone begins to blow the feather. The object of the game is not to allow the feather to go over your head or shoulders. With everyone blowing in all directions, the feather will eventually go over someone's head, and when that happens, the person is out. The game then continues with one less person. Each time someone is out, the group should move slightly closer together and adjust the sheet, grabbing more and more of it in their hands to maintain the shape of the circle and tautness of the sheet. The last person remaining is the winner.

This game will work with a Ping-Pong ball if you don't have a feather. It can also be done with everyone kneeling or sitting instead of standing.

46

Please Pass the Toothpick

Group size: 3 or more; the whole family, if possible

Age: 4 and up

Materials: 10 toothpicks for each person

---

*O*kay, *get out your* Donna Reed Show *reruns. We're going to* talk about table manners here, and not the version of manners most of us have become accustomed to, which I refer to at my house as table McManners!

This game should be played when your family is sitting down to dinner together. You might decide to do it on a special night when you have set a nice table, lit some candles, placed a centerpiece of fresh flowers on the table, or prepared an extra-sumptuous meal. If none of that rings a bell, it will also work when you're having hot dogs or frozen pizza, potato chips, Kool-Aid, and Ding-Dongs around the kitchen counter. Before you decide to play the game, however, it's a good idea to give your children some basic instructions regarding table manners. If you haven't done that yet, it's never too late to start!

Place 10 toothpicks at each person's place. Before you begin playing, tell your family you're going to see how well they know their table manners. Explain that every time someone notices another person *not* using proper manners, she can ask that person for one of his tooth-picks. He must give it up—cheerfully. When you have finished eating, the person with the most toothpicks is the winner. It might be fun to have a small treat or reward for the winner.

Be sure to set the proper tone for this game or it can turn into a battle. Emphasize from the beginning that this is for fun and learning, that there should be no fighting or whining during the game, and that people must give up their toothpicks willingly when "caught." You might even establish a rule that if someone argues about what they were or weren't doing, they have to give up two toothpicks. Also explain that you are only pointing out each other's mistakes as part of a learning activity. To do so in real life would not be proper and would be quite antisocial.

Here is a list of basic table manners to teach your family, which may be used for this game; or be creative and make up your own.

- No elbows on the table.

- Place your napkin in your lap.

- Wipe your mouth with your napkin, not on your hands or sleeves.

- Chew your food with your mouth closed.

- Say "please" when asking someone to pass an item and "thank you" when you get it.

- Do not talk with your mouth full.

- Use utensils, not your fingers, to eat food, except for items like bread, rolls, and other finger foods.

- Do not belch, slurp, or make other uncouth noises during dinner.

- Do not tip back your chair.

- Place your utensils on your plate between bites, and lay them neatly on the plate at the end of the meal.

- When you have finished, ask to be excused before leaving the table.

47
Yakety-Yak

Group size: 2 or more

Age: 5 and up

Materials: 2 paper cups, piece of string 12–20 feet long, 2 paper clips, 5 blank envelopes, marker

*P*oke a small hole in the bottom of the two paper cups. Thread one end of the string through the bottom of one cup and tie the string to the paper clip. The paper clip will be on the inside of the cup. Thread the other end of the string through the bottom of the other cup and tie it to a paper clip in the same manner.

Let two children hold one cup each and walk away from each other until the string is taut. Have one child cover his ear with the cup and the other child talk quietly into his cup. Then have them switch jobs. The string acts as a line of communication and the message is easily transferred from one child to the other.

Talk about communication with other people, the importance of speaking clearly and kindly to other children and adults. You might even use this to teach children how to respect their elders, referring to the fact that many times older people are hard of hearing and

have difficulty understanding when people use their normal tone of voice. It's
also a good time to discuss how important it is to communicate with honesty
and clarity, and to listen with empathy and understanding. Point out that
the string is free from interference and
therefore can carry the message without
interruption.

Now, on the outside of each envelope,
write a word or two describing something
that interferes with effective communication. These might be things like *self-
ishness, rudeness, interrupting, not
paying attention, being close-minded, illness, insecurity*, etc. These would need to be
adjusted according to the ages of the children. For
younger children they could be things like *yelling, lying,
whining, being selfish*.

While the two children are talking back and forth to
each other with their cups and string, hang the flap of
one of the labeled envelopes on the string. This will cut
down the children's ability to hear each other. Hang another envelope and then another, each time explaining
how these different qualities reduce the ability to communicate.

Try to give some examples within your family of a mis-
understanding between two people, and try to identify
the cause of the lack of communication. Emphasize the
importance of expressing your honest feelings when you
talk to other people, being a good listener, and using
words that are positive and uplifting instead of degrading.

One family I know of has a rule about brothers and sisters or parents who put each other down, a very common occurrence in families today and something that can simply become a bad habit. Whenever someone hears a put-down, the offender must say three "put-ups" about the person he has belittled. For instance, if Jacob says Tori is a "selfish brat," Jacob must then say three nice things about Tori before he can resume participating with the rest of the family or go back to his play. It's a good way to make kids aware of how much they inadvertently criticize each other.

PART TWELVE

Trust and Faith

For the children:

In spite of everything, I still believe that people are really good at heart.

—Anne Frank

For the parents:

Until I can risk appearing imperfect in your eyes, without fear that it will cost me something, I can't really learn from you.

—Rudolph Dreikurs

One day when my daughter Kelly was six, she brought her friend Tyler over to play. When they walked in, I said, "Hi, Tyler, what's new at your house?" Without a moment's hesitation she replied, "Who knows? At my house they *spell* everything!" I'm not sure whether Tyler's family needed a lesson in the value of being able to trust each other, or whether they had actually found a creative way around speaking the truth, but in any case, trust is an essential ingredient for any healthy family relationship, and one that can be improved with a little understanding and effort.

When a baby is born into a family, it might be comparable to being suddenly catapulted to Mars and being surrounded by strange creatures. The baby's immediate concerns are, "How safe am I? What's this place like? Can I trust these creatures?" The baby's early experiences tell him whether or not he can count on the people around him for friendly help in meeting his physical and emotional needs. This basic, safe, trusting feeling is essential for all children; without it, future healthy emotional development is thwarted.

Trust comes in many forms, but it always has something to do with keeping commitments, whatever they may be. When our children are young, we need to let them know where we're going and when we'll return. We need to prepare them ahead of time for the separation from us when they go to preschool or kindergarten. When children grow up knowing that if you tell them you'll be home from the movies by ten, you *will be*, it's much easier for them to understand why you might expect the same in return when they begin to go out as teenagers.

A climate of trust within a family says to a child, "You can count on me to help you meet your needs. I am not perfect but you can depend on my being honest with you, even about my imperfections. You can afford to be imperfect, too, and together we can try to strengthen our shortcomings. If I give you anything less than appropriate openness, I shortchange you. Masks aren't good enough because they keep us apart. You are safe with me."

As in most other aspects of life, in the areas of trust and faith our children will model their behavior on ours. If they see us trusting the world, having faith and hope in things not seen, they will develop a similar sense of trust. Stephanie Marston, the author of *The Magic of Encouragement*, says it this way: "Everything our children hear, see, and feel is recorded onto a cassette. Guess who is the big star in their movie? You are. What you say and, more important, what you do, is recorded there for them to replay over and over again. We all have videocassettes. Adults just have larger libraries of tapes available."

There are obviously some tricky aspects to teaching trust and faith to our kids. On the one hand, we want them to trust the world and have faith in the goodness of mankind. We want them to know that they can rely on us as their parents and that, generally, they can trust their friends, teachers, coaches, clergymen, etc. At the same time, however, we need to teach them the realities of life—that even good friends will let them down occasionally, that some teachers will have a different agenda than what's in the child's best interest, and that there are even a few bad people in the world who might try to harm them. So a delicate balance must be taught to our kids—one midway between an optimistic trust and a healthy skepticism.

For families with a religious background, trust is very closely associated with faith. Faith in God is something that seems to come naturally to most children, if they are encouraged at all in that direction. We can teach our children to trust in God, to have faith in His existence and in His love for us, and to have hope that He will direct us in ways that will ultimately bring us joy.

A simple, childlike faith is a lovely thing to behold, as is evidenced in this little girl's uninhibited heaven-bound letter: "Dear God, Thank you for the baby brother, but what I prayed for was a puppy.—Joyce." That kind of genuine candor would only be displayed toward someone very real to the child.

The following activities will give you ways to talk with your children about the importance of trust and faith. All of these can be related to trust among family members and friends, or they can transcend temporal affairs and be applied to more spiritual matters, if that has meaning to your family.

48
Dirt Dessert

Group size: 2 or more

Age: 3 and up

Materials: potted plant, tinfoil, Oreo cookies or chocolate wafers, spoon

*B*efore you begin this demonstration, cover the soil of any potted plant with small strips of tinfoil, removing some of the dirt at the top to leave a little space, if needed. Crush 6 to 8 Oreo cookies or 10 to 12 chocolate wafers (depending on the size of plant), or enough to cover all the tinfoil and make about one inch of chocolate "topsoil." This should be done without the children's knowing about it.

Begin by showing the pot and telling your child or family that it takes four things to make a plant grow: sun, air, water, and soil. This plant is healthy because it has had all four; it has been watered regularly and placed in the sunlight and fresh air, and was planted in rich potting soil full of vital nutrients.

Tell the children that the soil is so good and healthy, they could almost eat it, and ask whether someone would like to try a spoonful. This might take some coaxing, but try to convince them it will really taste good.

Tell them they can trust you because you would never do anything to harm them. You might even talk briefly about what trust is, and ask them about incidents in their life when they have learned to trust you as their parent.

After someone has tasted the "soil" and realizes what it is, explain that her trust and faith in you finally helped her believe you, knowing that, as her parent, you would never ask her to do something unhealthy. This trust gave her the courage to do what was asked.

Discuss the fact that often in life, we must rely on trust or faith instead of believing what we can merely see before us. A child won't always understand why she should obey certain rules and guidelines (going to school, wearing a bike helmet, eating healthy food, coming home before dark, helping a neighbor, or getting out of the ocean when she is asked), but she must understand that there are certain people in the world in whom she should develop enough trust to consistently believe them.

This might also be a good time to emphasize that not all people in the world can be trusted, and she should never feel compelled to do something against her own good judgment, especially if she is being encouraged by someone she doesn't know well.

If your family is religious, this activity can also be applied to having faith in God or a higher power. You can explain that although we cannot see God, we can learn to trust that He exists and that He will guide and protect us.

This exercise can also be done with a small, simple jar or glass and one seed, instead of a potted plant. Fill the jar with the cookie crumbs. Ask someone to plant the seed in the good potting soil. After she has used the spoon to make a hole and placed the seed in it, ask her to take a bite of the delicious, nutritious soil and then complete the activity as described.

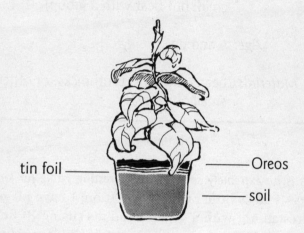

tin foil —————   ————— Oreos
                        ————— soil

49

Truth or Consequences

Group size: 2 or more (can be played with one child, but best with a group)

Age: 6 and up

Materials: beans, M&M's, toothpicks, or other small objects

*T*his is an extremely simple but interesting game for kids or adults. It takes little or no preparation; I have played it in a restaurant with a group of adults (using 10 fingers instead of 10 beans) or with a group of children riding in a car. Its main purpose is just the fun of "getting to know you" better, but it can also be related to the principle of trust and honesty.

Start out by giving each participant 10 M&M's, beans, marbles, pennies, or whatever other small objects you have around the house. If you're playing this at a party, M&M's or other small candies add to the fun of the game. One person begins by making a statement that must start with the words "I have never . . . " She must then think of something she has honestly never done (for children: played in a soccer game, gotten a "D" on a report card, worn lipstick, told a lie to a teacher, kissed a boy, ridden on a roller coaster, gotten an "A" in math, mowed a lawn, baked cookies, taken a candy bar from a store; for adults: been to Hawaii, been underweight, worn red tights, lied to my mother-in-law, done my child's homework, read two books in a week, graduated from college, fudged on my taxes, made a homemade pie).

After the statement has been made, everyone in the room who *has* done that activity or *has* had that experience must forfeit one of his or her candies to the person who made the original statement. (When playing without objects, everyone starts by holding up 10 fingers; each time they have to forfeit, they put 1 finger down.) The first person to give away all 10 objects is the winner —or loser, however you want to play it.

It's amazing what you can learn about people when they are honest, and because it's all done in fun, hopefully no one will be too sensitive about their own or their friends' truthful responses. For children, this game simply points out the difficulty, in certain situations, of being completely forthright, and for adults, the hilarious implications of the game are obvious.

50
Rising to the Top

Group size: 2 or more

Age: 5 and up

Materials: small clear jar with lid (like small pickle jar), 3 teaspoons metallic glitter, 3 tablespoons sand, 1–2 cups water, 3 tablespoons vegetable oil

*P*ut the glitter and the sand into the jar. Add the water and the oil. Screw the lid tightly onto the jar and hold it up for everyone to see. Tell the children that you will now separate the sand from the glitter without taking off the lid and without putting any tools into the jar. Ask them if they believe you can do it. Most children will probably not believe you, but encourage them to have faith in you—to believe in the possibility of things, even when they don't completely understand how they work.

Now tell the children that the jar can represent someone's life. Shake the jar vigorously and compare that to the trials and misfortunes that come into every life at some time (getting injured, struggling with schoolwork, having disagreements with family members or friends). After you stop shaking the jar, the sand will settle on the bottom and the glitter will rise to the top.

Compare the phenomenon to the fact that many times it is not until after we have gone through difficult times, and our faith has been tested, that the solution to our problem becomes clear. The trick is not to give up—to continue to believe, trust, and have faith even during our most difficult times.

51

Lean on Me

Group size: 2 or more

Age: 3 and up

Materials: blindfold, chairs, boxes, or other "obstacles" around the house

*T*here are two parts to this activity. The first part is very sim-*ple.* Blindfold a child, ask her to stand up, and have one parent stand directly in back of her. Tell the child that her father (or her mother) is right behind her. Ask her whether she trusts him to catch her if she falls. If the answer is no, the father should encourage her and promise he won't allow her to get hurt.

Instruct the child to put her arms straight out to the sides, keep her legs straight, and fall backward. At first, she will probably try to break her own fall by putting one leg back, but keep doing it over and over until she is confident and trusting enough so that she simply falls straight back into his arms. Take turns building trust in this way with other members of the family.

Talk about the idea that trust doesn't come naturally to children or adults. We learn to trust others through our experiences with them. We should not automati-cally trust people we don't know very well, but over time and through familiarity, we can usually learn to trust those close to us who are trustworthy. It's a good feeling for children and adults to be able to depend on each other, to rely on each other's word, to believe each other's promises. It's equally important for a child to learn to be trustworthy and dependable with others, so that she can expect the same in return. Ask why trust is an important quality within a family

The related part to this activity takes a little more setup, and is more effective with four or more people, but is still relatively simple. In another room or outside, place chairs, boxes, large toys, or other "obstacles" around the area to form an obstacle course. Blindfold one family member and have him walk into the area. Another member (ideally a parent) will guide him through the obstacle course, giving only verbal clues and no physical contact. Before he begins, tell him that someone he trusts will guide him through the course safely. Tell him there may be other outside influences as he goes, but that he should listen to his father's (or mother's) voice to know the best path to follow.

As the child begins the course, the parent should clearly direct him when to turn right or left, when to step over a box, when to stop. If there are other children present, they can act as "outside influences," trying to lead the blindfolded child astray by calling out wrong directions, tempts and taunts. The person going through the obstacle course must listen very carefully to be able to hear the correct coaching above the din. This can be a lot of fun for all involved, and it also teaches a valuable lesson. When the child has completed the course, try to emphasize how this experience relates to real life.

Depending on the age of the children, some enlightening conversation can come from the following questions. The questions can be simplified for young children:

• How is going through life a little like going through an obstacle course?

• In what ways are we "blindfolded" in life? Do we always know what's coming?

• Why is it important to have a few people whom you can always rely on and who will be there for you?

• Do you think those people would ever purposely lead you astray?

• Even though the people you trust will do their best to guide you, who makes the final decisions in the direction your life will take?

• What or who are some of the outside influences that might try to distract you from pursuing the most productive course?

• Why is it sometimes hard to know whom you can really trust, and why is it hard to consistently "hear" them?

• How can you be a more trustworthy friend or family member?

• If you have a religious persuasion, how does this activity relate to trust in God or a higher power?

52
Blind Faith

Group size: 3 or more

Age: 4 and up

Materials: blindfold, big bowl, 20–30 cotton balls, large plastic serving spoon

This is a fun game for kids, with or without the value lesson attached. Place the bowl on the floor (preferably a carpeted area) and scatter the cotton balls randomly around the bowl, some as far as three feet away from the bowl. Have the child sit or kneel on the floor in front of the bowl, blindfold him, and then hand him the spoon. His other hand must go behind his back. Tell the child he has one minute to scoop up as many cotton balls as possible with the spoon and put them in the bowl. After the minute, count the cotton balls in the bowl. Now scatter all the cotton balls again, have the next child repeat the process, and count how many he gets in. You can award a small prize to each participant, not just the one who gets the most cotton balls into the bowl.

Now discuss the idea that sometimes in life we do things we think are right without always knowing what the results will be. In a sense we are "blind" to the outcome of the act, and simply must trust that it will be for our good.

A farmer plants seeds every spring without knowing for sure the quality or abundance of the crop they will produce. As he covers the seeds with soil, he doesn't know whether they are good or not. He must wait patiently for several days or weeks to see whether they sprout. He also must trust that ultimately there will be enough rain and sunshine to make the seeds grow. If he didn't have any faith or trust, he would never plant the seeds to begin with.

When the child blindly scooped cotton into the bowl, he couldn't feel if he was doing any good or not—he didn't know if his efforts would be productive or fruitless. But he kept trying—he persevered in the darkness, trusting that some of his efforts would be rewarded.

Try to think of other examples when we must exhibit trust or faith in other people or in a higher power. Here are a few to get you started:

- You do your homework assignments, not fully understanding how you will need all that knowledge in your future life. You trust your teachers.

- You obey your parents when they tell you not to ride your bike beyond a certain point. You trust your parents.

- Your dad stops his car when a policeman holds up his hand and blows his whistle after there has been an accident. Your dad trusts the policeman and the law.

- Your baseball coach tells you that you should shorten your swing. You trust your coach.

- Your doctor tells you that you shouldn't go swimming for two weeks because of an ear infection. You trust your doctor.

- You say a prayer for protection because you're afraid during a thunderstorm. You trust in God.

If we can teach our children to believe, along with Anne Frank, that "in spite of everything . . . people are really good at heart," we will be giving them a great gift. They will experience the peace and confidence that results from an underlying faith in humankind.

Words to Live By

For Children

The best things in life aren't things.

Life sometimes gives you the test before you've had a chance to study the lesson.

You can count the seeds in an apple, but you can't count the apples in a seed.

Good manners sometimes means simply putting up with other people's bad manners.

Problems are opportunities in work clothes.

—HENRY KAISER

In spite of everything, I still believe that people are really good at heart.

—ANNE FRANK

True wealth is what you are, not what you have.

To say you're sorry does a funny thing, It warms the heart and cools the sting.

If you cannot do great things, do small things in a great way.

Your religion is what you do when the sermon is over.

You've got to stand for something, or you'll fall for anything.

You'll learn more about a road by traveling it than by consulting all the maps in the world.

What lies before you and what lies behind you are tiny matters compared to what lies within you.
—*EMERSON*

People are lonely because they build walls instead of bridges.
—*JOSEPH NEWTON*

Whenever you're blue
Find something to do
For somebody else
Who's sadder than you.

Parents don't make mistakes because they don't care, but because they care so deeply.
—*T. BERRY BRAZELTON*

There's always room for improvement; it's the biggest room in the house.
—*LOUISE LEBER*

Good actions are the invisible hinges on the doors of heaven.

For Parents

The journey of a
thousand miles
begins with one step.
—*LAO-TZU*

The only time we fail in
the home is when we give
up on each other.
—*MARVIN J. ASHTON*

The pessimist says, "I'll
believe it when I see it."
The optimist says, "I'll
see it when I believe it."
—*ROBERT SCHULLER*

Morality is what you
feel good after.
Immorality is what you
feel bad after.
—*ERNEST HEMINGWAY*

If you're going to leave
footprints in the sands of
time, you'd better wear
your working shoes.
—*LEGRANDE RICHARDS*

We have been so anxious
to give our children what
we didn't have that we
have neglected to give
them what we did have.

If love isn't taught
in the home, it is
almost impossible to
learn anywhere else.

What should not be
heard by little ears
should not be spoken
by big mouths.

Children who like
themselves like to
behave themselves.

Children spell love
T-I-M-E.

They may forget what you said, but they will never forget how you made them feel.

—CARL W. BUEHNER

A child with no limits is a child who will grow to hate freedom.

—FRED G. GOSMAN

The child benefits more from being valued than evaluated.

—DON DINKMEYER

Courage is the ability to go from one failure to another without losing your enthusiasm.

Nourish the mind as you would the body. The mind cannot survive on junk food.

—JIM ROHN

Every child comes with the message that God is not yet discouraged of man.

—RABINDRANATH TAGORE

A man travels the world over in search of what he needs and returns home to find it.

—GEORGE MOORE

Worry never robs tomorrow of its sorrow; it only saps today of its strength.

—A. J. CRONIN

Selected Bibliography

Briggs, Dorothy Corkille. *Your Child's Self-Esteem*. New York: Doubleday, 1975.

Church of Jesus Christ of Latter-Day Saints. *Family Home Evening Sourcebook*. Salt Lake City, Utah: Bookcraft, 1977.

Dosick, Wayne. *Golden Rules: The Ten Ethical Values Parents Need to Teach Their Children*. New York: HarperCollins, 1995.

Eisenberg, Arlene; Heidi E. Murkoff; and Sandee E. Hathaway, B.S.N. *What to Expect: The Toddler Years*. New York: Workman Publishing, 1994.

Eyre, Linda, and Richard Eyre. *Teaching Your Children Values*. New York: Simon & Schuster, 1993.

Garnett, Paul D. *Investigating Morals and Values in Today's Society*. Carthage, Ill.: Good Apple, 1988.

Ginsberg, Susan. *Family Wisdom: The 2,000 Most Important Things Ever Said About Parenting, Children, and Family Life*. New York: Columbia University Press, 1996.

Hample, Stuart, and Eric Marshall. *Children's Letters to God*. New York: Workman Publishing, 1991.

Heaton, Alma. *Tools for Teaching*. Salt Lake City, Utah: Bookcraft, 1979.

Selected Bibliography

Hollingsworth, Mary. *On Raising Children*. Dallas, Tex.: Word Publishing, 1993.

Lefgren, Beth, and Jennifer Jackson. *Power Tools for Teaching*. Salt Lake City, Utah: Bookcraft, 1988.

Luke, Susan. *Experiment upon the Word*. Salt Lake City, Utah: Covenant Communications, 1997.

Reuben, Steven Carr, Ph.D. *Raising Ethical Children*. Rocklin, Calif.: Prima Publishing, 1994.

Treseder, Terry W. *Teach Them to Love One Another*. Salt Lake City, Utah: Bookcraft, 1985.

Unell, Barbara C., and Jerry L. Wyckoff, Ph.D. *20 Teachable Virtues: Practical Ways to Pass on Lessons of Virtue and Character to Your Children*. New York: Berkley, 1995.

Weston, Denise Chapman, and Mark S. Weston. *Playwise: 365 Fun-Filled Activities for Building Character, Conscience, and Emotional Intelligence in Children*. New York: Jeremy P. Tarcher/Putnam Books, 1996.

Ziglar, Zig. *See You at the Top*. Gretna, La.: Pelican Publishing, 1981.

Index by Age Group

Index by Life Lesson

Index by Life Lesson

Ann Weil

Illustrated by Linda Sturm

STECK-VAUGHN
ELEMENTARY · SECONDARY · ADULT · LIBRARY

A Harcourt Company

www.steck-vaughn.com

ISBN 0-7398-5069-5

Copyright © 2003 Steck-Vaughn Company

Power Up! Building Reading Strength is a trademark of
Steck-Vaughn Company.

Printed in the United States of America.

2 3 4 5 6 7 8 9 LB 06 05 04 03 02

Contents

CHAPTER 1
Skateboard Sue

Nick stepped off his skateboard at the top of a big hill. He had walked up and down this hill many times, but he had never skated down it.

Nick had started skating six months ago. It was harder than he had thought it would be.

"Yee-ha!" Another skateboarder flashed past Nick. Long, black hair flew out from underneath a red helmet.

Nick knew it was Sue, even though he hadn't seen her face. Sue Chen was the best skateboarder at school. Everybody called her Skateboard Sue. Nick wished he could skate as well as she did.

Sue spun her skateboard around and stopped at the bottom of the hill.

"Are you walking or skating?" Sue yelled up at him.

Nick wasn't sure. Was he ready for this hill?

"Don't think about falling," Sue said. "Just be like the wind and blow down the hill!"

Nick took a deep breath. He stepped on his skateboard and pushed off. A moment later he was flying down the hill. He didn't try to stop at the bottom the way Sue did. Instead, he dragged one foot on the ground to slow himself down. The ride was over too soon. Nick thought about walking back up the hill and doing it again.

"Not bad." Sue's voice interrupted his thoughts.

"Thanks," Nick said.

"You should bend your knees a little more," she added.

Nick was glad that his friends weren't watching. They would have made fun of him. Nick was thrilled about skating down that hill without falling. He didn't even mind that Sue was telling him how to skate.

"Next time try to grind the curb on your way down," Sue said.

"I don't know how," Nick said.

"You jump up onto the curb so the concrete edge is between the wheels, on this part of the board." Sue pointed to the parts that held the wheels to the skateboard. "Those are called the trucks," she explained. "A grind is when one or both of the trucks scrape against the curb or against whatever you're skating on."

"I don't think I could do that," Nick said.

"I could show you how," Sue said.

Nick thought Sue was just being polite. Why would she want to skate with him? "No, that's okay. You don't have to do that," he said.

"It's no problem," Sue continued. "Let's meet on Sunday. How about noon at the 14th Street parking lot? Don't be late. I won't wait."

"Well, okay, if you're sure," Nick said. "I guess I could. . . ." Sue was already skating away.

Nick was at the parking lot five minutes early on Sunday. The lot was empty. It was the perfect place to practice.

As he waited for Sue, Nick did an "ollie." This jump was the basis of most skateboard tricks. He stood on the board with one foot toward the front and the other foot near the tail. Nick pushed down hard, smacking the tail of the board against the ground. This made the front of the board pop up into the air.

"Ready to do some curb grinds?" Sue asked as she skated up to him.

There was a curb along the side of the parking lot. Sue demonstrated the trick for Nick. Then, Nick tried it. The front of his skateboard hit the concrete.

"Keep trying. You'll get it soon," Sue said.

After a dozen tries, Nick finally got the trick.

"Great. Now we can really fly," Sue said. She pushed off hard and raced across the parking lot.

Sue skated around corners and jumped the curbs. Nick was out of breath when he caught up to her. She was standing under a sign on a fence that said "Caution."

"This is it," she said.

Nick looked around. What was Sue talking about? The sidewalk was closed. This was a construction area.

"We can't go in there." Nick pointed to a sign that said "Hard Hat Area."

"Why not?" Sue smiled. "We're wearing hard hats!" She tapped her helmet. "Workers aren't here on Sundays. We have the place to ourselves. You won't believe the size of the ramps in there. You can get some awesome air. Come on." She slipped through a hole in the fence and was gone.

Nick didn't follow her right away. This was his one big chance to learn how to skate. But was it worth the danger?

CHAPTER 2
Over the Top

"Hey, Nick! Are you coming?" Sue yelled.

Nick picked up his skateboard and followed Sue's voice.

The construction area took up a full city block. There were huge cement blocks and beams everywhere.

"Isn't this great?" Sue said. She was riding up and off a beam that rose out of the ground at an angle. She landed right next to Nick.

"That's called a pole jam," she explained. "Try it."

"I don't think I'm ready for that," Nick said. "Maybe I should try something easier." And less scary, he thought.

"Suit yourself," said Sue. "But I know you can do it. You just have to believe you can."

There were ramps everywhere. Some were wide enough for a truck. Others were as narrow as Nick's skateboard. He started with the wide ramps. He got up enough speed to do a few jumps. Then he practiced his grinds on a steel beam that was lying on the ground. He was concentrating so hard that he didn't notice Sue watching him.

"You could be really good, but you think too much," Sue said. "Give your mind a break. Use your feet instead." She picked up her skateboard and ran up a ramp. Then she jumped on her board and started down the ramp. When she reached a high speed, she turned toward the ramp's edge.

"Watch out!" Nick yelled, just as Sue skated off the edge of the ramp. She took off like a plane. She grabbed her skateboard with one

hand and held it in place under her feet. Nick
watched in fear as she flew through the air.
She was heading toward a stack of cement
blocks!

Sue touched down on top of the blocks.
Then she was in the air again, aiming straight
for a steel beam!

Sue arched her back. Her skateboard moved up in front of her body. Nick saw sparks fly as Sue's board hit the beam. She did a perfect grind down to the ground.

"Now that's a grind!" Nick said.

Sue smiled. "We'll work on slides next," she said. She ollied onto a low rail and slid down it on the wooden underside of her board, between the trucks. Nick watched her do the trick three times. Finally, he was ready to try it. He pushed off to get some speed.

"Grrrrr!"

"What's that?" Nick asked. He stopped skating and turned around.

"Grrrrr! Arf Arf ARF!"

A dog was growling and barking. It didn't sound friendly.

The noise was getting closer, too.

"Let's get out of here!" Sue yelled. She was already skating away.

Nick saw something moving behind the bags of cement. "What are you kids doing here?" yelled a security guard. He held a rope in one hand. There was a huge dog at the end of the rope. Nick hoped it was a strong rope.

He jumped on his board and followed Sue. He had never skated so fast in his life.

They ducked under a loose board in the fence and came out on the sidewalk.

"That was fun!" Sue said.

"That wasn't exactly my idea of a good time. We were almost dog food!" Nick's heart was still racing.

"We're not done yet. I know another place that's even better," Sue said as she skated ahead.

Nick hurried to keep up with her. He wanted to work on his slide.

He saw Sue skate around a corner. But when Nick turned the same corner, he found himself in a dead-end alley.

Sue was nowhere in sight.

CHAPTER 3
Adventure Underground

Now what? Nick wondered. Had she left him? He was about to turn back and go home.

Sue's head popped up from an open manhole. "Let's go!"

She was standing on a ladder. Nick looked down into the darkness. "You're kidding, right? I'm not going down there."

"Come on! It'll be fun," Sue said.

"No way! That's a sewer. It smells bad and it's dirty."

"How do you know?" Sue asked. "Have you ever been inside a city sewer before?"

"Well. . . no," Nick answered. "But I've heard that there are alligators down there."

Sue laughed. "You believe that?"

"It's true! A friend of mine told me. Kids get these baby alligators as pets. When the alligators get too big, the kids flush them. The alligators are washed into the sewers, and they grow really huge. There are probably hundreds of them down there."

"You worry too much," Sue said. She was already climbing down the ladder.

Nick couldn't believe that Sue was really going to skateboard in a city sewer. But he had thought going into the construction area was a bad idea. It had turned out to be a lot of fun.

Nick climbed down the ladder after Sue.

At the bottom of the ladder, there was a huge, dark tunnel. Sue was just a shadow ahead of him. It wasn't at all like Nick had thought it would be. It didn't smell bad. Grates above their heads let in air and light.

Sue ran up the side of the tunnel. Then she hopped onto her skateboard and skated down to pick up some speed. She skated up the other side of the tunnel until she was almost vertical. Then she flipped her skateboard and skated down again.

Nick copied her moves. This isn't so hard, he thought. They skated like this for a few minutes. Nick was having fun, but Sue seemed a little bored.

"Where do these tunnels go?" Nick shouted.

"Water drains into the tunnels so the streets don't flood," Sue explained. "These tunnels go on for miles, as far as the river."

"Is that where we're going?" Nick asked.

"No," Sue answered.

"So…where are we going?" Nick was beginning to get nervous.

"It's a surprise," Sue said. "Don't worry. You'll love it."

Nick watched Sue do a full loop around the inside of the tunnel. How did she get enough speed to do that? he wondered.

Nick pushed off, trying to get up more speed. He felt something touch his foot. He looked down.

He couldn't believe what he saw.

Hundreds of rats were running around the tunnel. Some were crawling onto his skateboard. They were only inches from his legs.

"Sue!" he yelled. "Rats!" Nick felt like he was going to throw up.

"Just keep moving," she said. "They'll get out of your way."

The rats scattered as Nick skated past them.

"We're almost there!" Sue yelled.

Almost where? Nick wondered. And do I really want to get there?

Nick followed Sue up a ladder. He thought any place would be better than the sewer. When they got to the top of the ladder, they were inside a subway station.

Nick saw Sue skating toward some stairs that led even farther underground.

"Yee-ha!" Sue yelled as she skated off the edge of the top stair. One hand held her skateboard. The other waved for Nick to follow.

Without even thinking, Nick ollied up onto the hand rail next to the stairs. He did a slide down to the bottom.

"See," Sue said. "You can really skate when you stop worrying. Now let's do some grinds on the train tracks." Sue skated toward the edge of the platform.

"Uh…Sue…what if a train comes?" Nick asked, still standing on the platform.

"No trains, no people. They don't use this station anymore."

Just as Sue finished talking, there was a rumbling sound. The ground began to shake.

"Are you sure about that?" Nick asked.

Sue skidded to a stop. "I could be wrong." They heard a train whistle blow.

"Let's get out of here!" Sue shouted over the noise.

It was late afternoon when Nick and Sue climbed out of the manhole into the light of day. They had spent many hours under the city. For a few seconds, Nick couldn't see. The sun was really bright after the darkness of the tunnel.

Then he saw the police officer. "I've been looking for you two," she said.

CHAPTER 4
Skateboard City

Nick had never been in trouble with the police. What if he went to jail?

The officer took a phone from her belt. "Hello . . .yes, I found two of them. I'll bring them right over. You can call their parents when we get there." She said goodbye and hung up.

"Do you really need to call our parents?" Nick asked.

"Yes, we need to call your parents," the officer said. "You two could get hurt down there or lost."

Nick said, "We promise not to go there again."

But the police officer just shook her head and said, "Come with me."

As he followed the officer, Nick watched Sue ollie on and off the curb. She didn't seem scared at all. Nick carried his skateboard.

They followed the police officer into the Central Park Zoo.

Sue whispered to Nick, "This is a great place to skate. We can slide down those hand rails."

"How can you think about skating now?" Nick asked. "We're in big trouble!"

"You worry too much," Sue said.

The officer took them to a large, brick building. The sign in front read "Parks Department."

The officer led them down a hall. She knocked on a door. A young woman opened it. A man was standing behind her.

"Come in," she said.

The officer held the door open for Nick and Sue.

The young woman said, "I'm Angela Ward. And this is John Roy."

"Glad to meet you," Mr. Roy said, smiling at Nick and Sue. "We asked the police to help us find some skateboarders. We're designing a new skateboarding park. We were hoping you'd help us."

The police officer said, "They need your help, too. I found them skateboarding in the sewer. A park is just what they need." She turned to leave.

"So, why are you going to call our parents?" Nick asked Mr. Roy.

Mr. Roy answered, "We just want to get their permission for you to talk to us."

Nick was relieved. He and Sue wrote down their phone numbers. As Mr. Roy made the calls, Ms. Ward showed Nick and Sue the plans for the new skate park.

Sue looked disappointed.

"You don't skate, do you?" she said to Ms. Ward.

"Well, no…," Ms. Ward answered. "But we've studied skate parks all over the country."

"This one looks boring," Sue said.

"Well, what would you like to see in a skate park?" Ms. Ward asked Sue.

Sue thought for a few seconds. "Maybe you could have different areas. One could be like a construction area with ramps and steel beams and cement blocks to jump over. Another could be like a subway station. Kids could grind the rails and slide off the benches."

"Like where we were skating this morning," Nick said. "Only safer."

"And nobody would worry about getting in trouble," Sue said. "You could make the park as challenging as the real world of the city, or what's under it!"

Ms. Ward and Mr. Roy wrote down everything Sue said. "These are great ideas!" Mr. Roy said. "Thanks for your help!"

"Do you think they'll use your ideas?" Nick asked Sue as they were leaving.

"Probably not," Sue answered. She did a slide down the hand rail next to the seal pond.

Nick said, "But Ms. Ward seemed really interested in what you were saying."

"I'll make you a deal. If they use my ideas, I'll do a back flip at the new park," Sue said with a smile. "If they don't, you do the back flip."

Nick almost ran back into the building to beg Ms. Ward to use Sue's ideas!

Many months later, Nick and Sue went to the opening of Skateboard City. They had been invited to be the first to skate in the park.

When they got to the park, they saw the mayor up on a high platform. He was speaking into a microphone. "We are pleased to welcome all of you to the newest, largest skate park in the country!"

The crowd cheered.

"And now, the person who made all this happen," the mayor said. "Angela Ward!"

Ms. Ward stepped up to the microphone. "Thank you. But we really should thank a young skateboarder named Sue Chen." Ms. Ward looked into the crowd. "Sue? Are you here?"

Nick gave Sue a little push. But Sue wouldn't go up to the platform alone. She grabbed Nick's sleeve. The two of them climbed the steps to join Ms. Ward.

"Sue, thank you for helping with the design of this park," Ms. Ward said. "We want you and Nick to be the first to try it."

Sue and Nick jumped onto their boards and skated into the park. The crowd followed.

There were "Oooohs" and "Ahhhhs" as everybody saw the amazing park for the first time. It had been built exactly the way Sue had described it to Ms. Ward.

Nick and Sue sped through the park doing ollies, slides, and grinds. Nick had no trouble keeping up with Sue.

"Don't forget our deal," he reminded her.

With the crowd watching, Skateboard Sue did a perfect back flip.